EXOTIC
BETTING

How to Make the Multihorse, Multirace Bets
That Win Racing's Biggest Payoffs

STEVEN CRIST

DRF PRESS
New York

Published by
Daily Racing Form Press
100 Broadway, 7th Floor
New York, NY 10005

ISBN: 1-932910-92-1
Library of Congress Control Number: 2006921697

Jacket design by Chris Donofry
Text design by Neuwirth & Associates

Printed in the United States of America

All entries, results, charts and related information provided by

821 Corporate Drive • Lexington, KY 40503-2794 Toll Free (800) 333-2211 or
(859) 224-2860; Fax (859) 224-2811 • Internet: www.equibase.com

The Thoroughbred Industry's Official Database for Racing Information

CONTENTS

ACKNOWLEDGMENTS

A FUNNY THING happened on the way to this volume. Five years ago, in 2001, I began to write a handicapping book, but it somehow turned into a memoir of a career in the racing industry that was published in 2002 as *Betting on Myself: Adventures of a Horseplayer and Publisher.*

That unexpected change of direction was probably a fortuitous one. At the time, I was playing the races with far less dedication and enthusiasm than usual. Acquiring the *Daily Racing Form* in 1998 and trying to turn it into a better newspaper and wagering tool had been a longtime goal and passion, but overseeing its daily operations and impersonating a chief executive officer was a job that left me little time for my own handicapping and betting. This followed a stint from 1994 to 1997 where I joined the circus I had previously written about and worked as a racetrack vice president, a hitch during which my employers preferred that I not bet at all. So I had been out of serious action for the better part of a decade.

I returned to daily handicapping after *Betting on Myself* was published, and then the *Form* was sold in 2004 to new investors who asked me to stay on in an advisory and writing capacity, a dream job that allowed me to return to the full-throttle horseplaying of a decade earlier. In my time away from the trenches, the game's trend toward exotic betting had accelerated rapidly. I realized that the handicapping book that perhaps needed to be written was not another one about selecting winning horses but one about how to bet one's selections, however they are arrived at, in the burgeoning exotic pools that had always been the focus of my own wagering.

No book gets to readers without the generous assistance of many people beyond the author. So I would like to thank Dan Black, Brent Diamond, and Craig Klosk of *Daily Racing Form* and The Wicks Group for giving me the time and latitude to write the book I wanted; Chris Donofry for his excellent cover and design; Dean Keppler of DRF Press for his ongoing help and patience; Maggie Estep, Tim O'Leary, Andy Serling, and Mike Watchmaker for their time and suggestions after reading the first draft; and my partner and editor, Robin Foster, for her invaluable attention and improvements to the manuscript.

April 2006

BEYOND THE
ONE-HORSE BET

THIS IS NOT a book about how to pick winners at the race-track. Selecting the horses who are likely to run well in a given race is of course essential to any wagering success, but it is only half the battle. The rest of it is in how you bet them, a far more neglected topic in both the literature of Thoroughbred handicapping and the skill set of the modern horseplayer.

The most common lament among unsuccessful racetrack gamblers is that they are excellent handicappers but lousy bettors and money-managers. This is only partially correct. In truth, many of them are lousy handicappers too. It is easier to blame a lack of technical expertise at executing wagers than it is to admit to a lack of analytical skills. Still, it is also true that most racetrack bettors spend far more time thinking about who will win a race than on how to bet a race.

Handicapping and betting are inextricably linked, now more than ever. In an earlier era when the only way to wager on the races was to settle on a preferred horse and bet him to win, place, or show, selecting your horse was about all there was to it. Today, with literally hundreds of options and permutations on the modern racetrack wagering menu, choosing the most advantageous and appropriate betting pool and structuring a wager are just as important.

These relatively new wagers are also the area of greatest opportunity in the game today. Selecting a single horse to win, and trying to pick winners often enough or at sufficiently generous odds to show a profit over time, has become harder than ever. Even the most precise sharpshooters, willing to sit on their hands race after race until a favorable situation arises, no longer enjoy the advantages they once did.

In racetrack wagering, the competition comes from the other horseplayers, a group that has undergone significant change over the last generation or two. Many of the game's most casual fans, who once happily fattened the pools with uninformed wagers on names and numbers, have largely been lured away by the blinking lights of casinos and the jackpot payoffs of state lotteries. The remaining customers not only must be better than their fellow horseplayers, but also must do so in an Information Age where many of the old advantages afforded by proprietary knowledge have disappeared. They also must overcome a house edge that takes a punitive 15 to 25 percent off the top of the betting pool for expenses before the rest is distributed to those holding winning tickets.

It is a daunting prospect, but there is hope.

Thirty years ago, over 90 percent of the wagering on horse races was in "straight" betting—mostly win betting, with its watered-down cousins place and show available for the fainter of heart. Today, however, that has nearly flip-flopped: Over 70 percent of the $15 billion wagered annually on American races is now spent on bets once considered so peculiar, and even disreputable, that they are still known as exotics—daily doubles, exactas, trifectas, superfectas, pick threes, pick fours, pick sixes, and other variations. All of them involve betting on either the extended order of finish in a race—the 1-2, 1-2-3, or even 1-2-3-4 finishers—or on the winners of consecutive races in advance.

Wagers in these pools exceed $10 billion annually, a robust and growing number, but the vast majority of bettors still spend too much time trying to zero in on the single most likely winner of a race and too little time understanding and exploiting the complexities and opportunities inherent in these wagers.

In the world of poker, it is often said that good players don't need good cards to win. Their understanding of the game's percentages and of their opponents' shortcomings is advantage enough. The situation is similar in modern race-track betting. The small number of regular winners do not pick an unusually high percentage of winning horses, and they are no likelier than anyone else to have a correct opinion on who will win the Kentucky Derby.

In fact, they have plenty of good opinions, but they are the types of perceptions that did not have an exploitable outlet in the old days of win, place, and show betting. The opinion is less likely to be that a particular horse looks like a certain winner than that a certain type of race is liable to have either a very formful or a very chaotic result; that the public is absolutely right about a deserving favorite but dead wrong about who is the second most likely winner; or that a particular kind of shaky favorite is unlikely to finish in the top three or four if he doesn't win.

It used to be that such perceptions were analytically interesting but of little value in the inevitable narrowing of a field to the single horse most deserving of a win bet. In the world of exotic betting, however, they are the foundation for investments that can yield payoffs literally hundreds or thousands of times greater than those available to the straight bettors of yore.

Even for those who play the races only occasionally and with a far greater emphasis on short-term enjoyment than long-term profit, the exotics are well worth exploring. Beyond their possible financial rewards, they are just plain entertaining. They also can reward unconventional and creative thinking in ways that a win or place bet never could.

The Rise of the Exotics

For almost as long as there have been horses, people have raced them and wagered on the outcome. The endeavor has almost always been defined with a single objective: to identify the most likely winner of the race and bet on him.

This is not mere gambling or speculation. Horse racing has always been both alike and quite different from other wagering propositions such as dice, cards, or roulette. It is similar insofar as it is an event that ends with the generation of a "winning" number. Take 10 horses, put a numbered cloth over each of them, and at the end of a race, number 1 or 3 or 10 will finish first, just as a turn of the card, a roll of a die, or a spin of the wheel will end with a nine of spades, double sixes, or 23 black.

The crucial difference is that while the result of the number-generation among inanimate objects is entirely random (unless the game is rigged through a tilted wheel or loaded dice), the result of the horse race has an undeniable element of predictability. Through knowledge and analysis of the horses, their previous performances, and literally hundreds of other factors, it is possible to predict the outcome of a race at a much higher rate than the outcome of a random event.

There are six sides to a die and a precisely 1 in 6 chance of predicting which one will end up on top. It is entirely impossible to make an educated guess as to whether a one or a six is more likely, and this is why there is no such thing as a skilled or a winning craps player. In six-horse races, however, the betting public does roughly twice as well, picking the winner about 35 percent of the time as opposed to the 16.67 percent rate for forecasting a dice roll.

Until the last 30 years, centuries of horse-race handicapping and wagering were focused almost exclusively on honing this element of predictability in search of the winning horse. Then, as now, there were people who bet nothing but favorites and others who backed longshots in search of a higher return, but wagering had one focus: the performance of a single horse whom the bettor had selected.

As recently as 1970, over 90 percent of racetrack wagering consisted of win, place, and show bets (known in the industry as WPS and pronounced "whips") on individual horses. When Secretariat won the 1973 Kentucky Derby, those were the only available wagers at Churchill Downs. Race results could be summarized in three brief lines of agate type in a newspaper:

	Win	**Place**	**Show**
1 Secretariat	$5.00	$3.20	$3.00
5 Sham		$3.20	$3.00
8 Our Native			$4.20

Those who had selected Secretariat to win got back $5 for every $2 they had wagered, a $3 profit for every $2 invested, and that 150 percent return on investment was the highest available on the race. If you had hedged your bet a little and taken $2 on Secretariat both to win and to place, your $4 investment returned $8.20 ($5 + $3.20), two dimes better than doubling your money. If you backed Sham to win, you lost. If you had bet $2 "across the board" on Sham ($2 to win, $2 to place, and $2 to show), you invested $6 and got back $6.20, a 3 percent profit comparable to the annual return on a municipal bond.

By 2005, two things had changed. First, most daily newspapers no longer carried the agate results of races. In those that still did, though, the three lines of WPS payoffs were now merely the beginning to a long list of payoffs reflecting a new universe of available wagers. Thirty-two years after Secretariat, the betting results from the Kentucky Derby looked like this:

	Win	Place	Show
10 Giacomo	$102.60	$45.80	$19.80
18 Closing Argument		$70.00	$24.80
12 Afleet Alex			$ 4.60

$2 Exacta 10-18: $9,814.80
$2 Trifecta 10-18-12: $133,134.80
$1 Superfecta 10-18-12-17: $864,253.50
$2 Daily Double 9-10: $1,973.40
$2 Oaks/Derby Double 5-10: $595.20
$2 Pick Three (8-9-10): $21,335.20
$2 Pick Four (1-8-9-10): $164,168.60
$2 Pick Six (5-5-1-8-9-10), 5 correct: $11,228.20; carryover pool: $471,588

WPS bets attract a higher percentage of the action on the Derby than almost any other race of the year, given that there are so many once-a-year racegoers unschooled in exotics participating in the betting pools. Even on Derby Day, though, WPS bettors had become a minority by 2005. Of the $97 million wagered on the race, only $42 million was in WPS pools, with the other $55 million on the "exotic" bets that had barely existed a generation earlier.

An even more striking example involves the slightly higher $112 million wagered on the eight Breeders' Cup races October 29, 2005, at Belmont Park. Here, only $38.7 million (34.6 percent) was wagered in the straight pools, while the remaining $73.3 million (65.4 percent) was wagered on the exotics, which comprised eight exactas, eight trifectas, eight superfectas, six pick threes, two pick fours, and a pick six.

At the first Breeders' Cup 21 years earlier in 1984, about 65 percent of the handle had been in the straight pools, with the few exotics—five exactas and a daily double—accounting for just 35 percent of the day's wagering.

The literature of handicapping is remarkably lean on the seemingly crucial issue of how to play these new bets that account for a majority of the $15 billion wagered on American horse races each year. For every 10 books or articles about how to select winning horses, there is perhaps one self-published pamphlet on the philosophy or the mechanics of executing wagers. Racetracks have historically explained and promoted these bets only by regularly printing small charts in their track programs outlining the cost of "boxing" or "wheeling" horses, two primitive methods of playing exotics that are as inefficient and unrewarding as they are popular.

Horseplayers are bombarded with selections and with conflicting theories and methods of making picks, but are largely left on their own to figure out which bets to make and how to make them. Many players lurch from one kind of exotic bet to another, tantalized by the different challenges and potentially larger payouts, but do so without a good understanding of how the bets really work and which ones are appropriate to their individual circumstances—their abilities and their bankrolls.

In the broad sweep of American horseplaying history, exotic betting is in its relative infancy. For the first half of the 20th century, few tracks offered anything more exotic than a single daily double, a bet requiring you to pick the winners of the afternoon's first two races in advance, introduced as a promotional gimmick to get patrons to arrive promptly for the entire program. Exactas, requiring selection of the first two finishers in a race, became commonplace by the 1970's, and the pick six, requiring six straight winners in advance, debuted at American tracks in the early 1980's. It was really only in the 1990's, however, that trifectas became available on virtually every race, that superfectas found their way onto the betting menu, and that pick threes and pick fours became ubiquitous.

The sudden rise of the exotics in the late 20th century, after hundreds of years of predominantly straight wagering, corresponds precisely to the proliferation of competing forms of gambling. State lotteries offering life-changing jackpots began in the 1970's, and the opening of Resorts International in Atlantic City, New Jersey, in 1976 marked the beginning of a massive spread of casino gambling beyond the borders of Nevada. At this writing, there are lotteries in 37 states and casinos in 26.

In the face of big lottery and slot-machine payoffs, getting $6.20 for $2 suddenly seemed far less interesting. Other forms of parimutuel wagering, particularly greyhound racing and jai alai, were far quicker to embrace exotic bets and their higher payoffs than the Thoroughbred-racing industry, which largely fought them for as long as possible.

Thoroughbred track executives at the time feared that the exotics would cheapen the pageantry of their ancient "Sport of Kings" and might bankrupt their customers, particularly the $2 bettors who might now have to invest more money by buying multiple combinations. Charles Cella, the longtime owner of Oaklawn Park in Hot Springs, Arkansas, adopted "No Gimmicks!" as an anti-exotics track slogan in the 1980's, vowing that Oaklawn would never offer anything racier than one daily double each afternoon. California tracks actually tried to price their smaller customers out of playing exotics by putting a higher minimum on them. At that first Breeders' Cup at Hollywood Park in 1984, exactas were a minimum $5 bet per combination.

"We're trying to save the customers from themselves," said Cliff Goodrich, then the president of Santa Anita Park.

By 2005, Cella still owned Oaklawn and Goodrich was the president of Arlington Park. Both tracks, as well as those in California and almost everywhere else, were now offering a full menu of exotics, including superfectas at a 10-cent minimum bet.

In addition to belatedly recognizing the public appetite for the exotics, track officials had two other reasons to embrace them. First, they found that they were able to win government approval for increasing their profits by raising the rate of taxation on these bets, an issue that will be discussed at greater length in the next chapter. Second, exotics proved to be a solution to, or at least a distraction from, the ongoing problem of increasingly small and uncompetitive fields of horses in American racing.

Despite improvements in veterinary care and track maintenance, horses are making fewer starts per year than they did a generation ago, and the average field size has shrunk from

10 to 8 starters per race. Even that declining number is somewhat inflated because of the profusion of large fields of maidens in many jurisdictions, meaning that there are plenty of four- and five-horse fields nowadays. These short fields are especially unappetizing win-bet propositions because of the greater likelihood of a heavy favorite at extremely low odds and the smaller chance that the betting public will overlook the merits of any contender and allow him to go off at a generous price.

Exotic wagering thus became a necessity for the tracks in order to keep their betting somewhat appealing as field size steadily decreased. Having an exacta turns a race with only five win-bet choices into the equivalent of a 20-horse win-bet field because there are 20 possible exacta combinations. The good news for exotics players is that just as the win bettors are likely to allow one or more horses in a 20-horse field to go off at too big a price, there is frequently similar value to be found in the exacta pool of only a five-horse race.

The Exotic Opportunity

What the executives who initially resisted the exotic onslaught misunderstood was that exotic bets would not necessarily force small bettors or anyone else to bet any more or less. The bettor who used to spend $10 or $12 a race betting $10 to win or $4 across the board might now spend the same amount of money "boxing" three horses or keying one horse over five or six others in a $2 exacta.

This is how the majority of bettors began playing exotics, buying however many combinations they could afford at their previous levels of straight betting, and probably getting the same kind of total return but with better-sounding individual payoffs. Instead of betting $12 to win and place on a favorite, and getting back $60 for $24 if the horse paid $6.60 to win and $3.40 to place, a player might now box four horses for the same $24 (buying 12 combinations at $2 each) and perhaps hit a $60 exacta. This was hardly slot-machine territory, but a $60 payoff sounded grander than $6.60 and $3.40.

Even today, many players seem not to have progressed beyond this level. Minimums eventually dropped from $5 to $2 and now $1 in most exotic bets, allowing the purchase of more combinations in trickier pools, such as the trifecta, which requires you to select the first three finishers in a race rather than the exacta's first two.

The relative newness of exotic wagers, and the resulting confusion and lack of expertise in the betting marketplace, represent an ongoing opportunity and a reason for the modern player to sharpen his skills with these pools. An insight or advantage in any investment market remains valuable only until the competition—in this case, the other players, who set the odds through their bets—figures it out. Economists call a market "efficient" when the prices reflect the actual probabilities that various outcomes will occur.

WPS betting is generally an efficient market. The public at large is extremely good at identifying the most likely winner of a race. There are no great mysteries about which horse is going to go off as the favorite, and year after year, over hundreds of thousands of races, 2-1 shots win more often than 3-1 shots, who win more often than 6-1 shots, and so on. There are no particular sweet spots or aberrations because the question of who is the most likely winner has essentially been solved.

Identifying such horses is simply not the most meaningful skill anymore, especially in the face of the information explosion that has revolutionized handicapping in recent decades. The modern horseplayer has unprecedented, instantaneous access to sophisticated speed figures that equalize time over different distances and surfaces, lifetime past performances crammed with relevant historical data, video race replays, breeding and trainer databases, and other analytical tools that were once the exclusive province of obsessive devotees who crafted their own ratings and laboriously maintained handwritten records.

While all this new information has not solved every puzzle, and favorites win at roughly the same rate they did 50 years ago, the opportunities for making highly profitable conventional bets have almost certainly diminished. A winning 10-1 shot of yesteryear might have actually had the best speed figure in the race, or the connections or breeding to excel in a specific situation, facts known to only a handful of canny experts. Today such a horse might be 4-1 at best, vastly decreasing the chances for the occasional big betting scores that lead to profitability.

One-horse betting made far more sense in the earlier era, when exclusive access to proprietary information alone might have provided a likely winner at a big WPS price. Perhaps 50 years from now, the betting public will have figured out optimal strategies for the exotics, but for now it is largely an unmined wilderness, particularly in the newer bets involving three or more horses. Overlays—payoffs that are higher than they should be—abound in the exotic pools because many players approach them as nothing but more complicated win bets rather than entirely different entities that require entirely different approaches. Simply put, the exotic pools are still inefficient markets, and their inefficiency increases as the bets become more complex and the potential for big payoffs increases.

Such payoffs are necessary for success. I have never heard of, let alone seen the mansion belonging to, a horseplayer who supports himself by grinding away at short-priced win bets day after day. Handicapping books used to urge people to try to pick 35 percent winners at an average $6 win mutuel, which would produce a 5 percent profit over time. I doubt the existence of such bettors as much as I feel sorry for those who have turned their horseplaying into such an unimaginative and joyless enterprise.

Most of today's winning players follow a different blueprint for long-term profitability: making the occasional score through exotic wagering, and not giving it all back before the next such happy occasion comes along. A score does not necessarily mean the $864,253.50 superfecta on the 2005 Kentucky Derby. It might be a $6,000 pick six, a $600 trifecta, or even that $60 exacta that once seemed exotic.

In all of these cases, though, the score was ultimately achievable because of the very nature of an exotic bet: *the opportunity to receive significantly higher odds than you deserve by betting on more than one thing at once—and by betting on more interesting and rewarding things than who is the likeliest first-place finisher in a single race.*

Choices, Choices, Choices

In Grandfather's day, once you had picked your preferred horse, the only decision was whether to bet him to win or to hedge a bit with a place and/or show bet so you'd get a little something back if he ran second or third. (Place and show bets are almost always bad ideas, and repeated studies have shown that WPS bettors are cheating themselves out of long-term profits by not betting solely to win.) In any case, a bettor did not have to spend a great deal of time deciding which types and amounts of wagers to execute.

Today, with so many options and permutations on the modern racetrack wagering menu, the horseplayer faces dozens of decisions. Let's say you want to bet on a horse in the ninth and final race of the day. You might have 10 options as to how and where to play him: In the three WPS pools, in the ninth-race exacta, trifecta, or superfecta, or as the last leg of a late double, pick three, pick four, and pick six.

Each pool offers both general and situation-specific advantages and drawbacks that need to be considered coldly, in terms of both your handicapping abilities and your personal finances. While the game may have been less interesting and rewarding in the WPS-only era, it was both simpler and, in a sense, more fair. If you had as little as $6 to play a race, you could make the minimum $2 bet in all three pools, and you had the same opportunity and leverage as someone betting $60 or $6,000. The richest and poorest players at the track stood shoulder to shoulder, with the same rooting interest and equal access to cashing tickets.

Exotic betting has changed all that in ways that the majority of players may not adequately comprehend. That same $6 won't go very far in even the simplest of multiple wagers, such as daily doubles and exactas, and it is folly to invest so little in anything more complicated, such as a trifecta or pick four—simply because even with the lower $1 minimum on most exotic bets, $6 buys you an inadequately small number of combinations in pools with massive numbers of possible outcomes. Consider the possible number of winning combinations in eight-horse races, the current average field size in American racing, for each type of bet:

Win	8 combinations
Quinella	28 combinations
Exacta	56 combinations
Double	64 combinations
Trifecta	336 combinations
Pick Three	512 combinations
Superfecta	1,680 combinations
Pick Four	4,096 combinations
Pick Six	262,144 combinations

In an eight-horse race with 1,680 possible superfecta combinations, holding only 6 or even 12 or 24 of them doesn't give you much coverage. Even if your circumstances allow you to bet more than $24, you will be at a huge disadvantage in an extended multirace wager such as the pick four, where there are 4,096 possible combinations over four eight-horse races, a number that increases to 10,000 with four 10-horse fields and to 38,416 with a quartet of 14-horse fields on a Breeders' Cup card.

Before you slam this book shut at the prospect of finding the winning needle in such large haystacks, it's not entirely as daunting as the possible-outcome numbers above might seem. Let's say that your handicapping skills allow you to eliminate just three of the runners in each eight-horse field from consideration. You have only reduced the number of possible win bets by 37.5 percent, from eight to five, but look what happens in the other pools:

	Eight Contenders	Five Contenders
Win	8 combinations	5 combinations
Quinella	28 combinations	10 combinations
Exacta	56 combinations	20 combinations

	Eight Contenders	Five Contenders
Double	64 combinations	25 combinations
Trifecta	336 combinations	60 combinations
Pick Three	512 combinations	125 combinations
Superfecta	1,680 combinations	120 combinations
Pick Four	4,096 combinations	625 combinations
Pick Six	262,144 combinations	15,625 combinations

Those haystacks look a lot smaller now, and this highlights a key point common to all exotic wagers: Eliminating horses from contention can be as important and valuable a skill as making fine-line decisions about which of the likely contenders is the likeliest winner. Throw out three horses in an eight-horse field and you still have five win bets to choose from, but do the same thing in a superfecta and you have eliminated over 90 percent of the possible winning combinations. As we shall see when we examine each type of bet, this is the sort of unconventional thinking that makes these wagers quite different from win betting.

Even in the universe of fewer combinations after eliminating noncontenders, the more exotic exotics still offer enough possible outcomes that a player buying just 24 or 48 of them is virtually naked. Bettors putting in substantially more money than average are not necessarily better handicappers, but they have two advantages—one that cannot be mimicked by smaller players, but one that can. First, they simply have more combinations. Second, they receive higher payoffs than they should on many winning combinations that are only mildly difficult, because their payoffs are inflated by small players who overbet the most obvious combinations due to their limited means.

For example, there are 512 possible pick-three outcomes for picking in advance the winners of three eight-horse races

(8 x 8 x 8). Of those 512 combinations, the most heavily bet 25 or so will be overbet because these same combinations will be on the tickets of so many of the smaller players, many of whom are combining the two or three obvious favorites in each race. This depresses the odds and payoffs on these most-favored combinations while inflating them on the next most logical group of possible outcomes, simply because the small players are afraid to leave out favorites and then cannot afford to go deeper.

An average player can't do anything about the fact that others with deeper pockets can outspend him, but he can avoid playing these overbet combinations by deliberately excluding them from his plays, a topic to which we shall repeatedly return in this volume.

At this writing there is some hope on the horizon for a change in wagering practices that would make some of these bankroll issues moot: lowering the minimums for some exotic bets, an eccentric cause I have been championing in recent years, which has met some success with the widespread adoption of 10-cent superfectas in American racing.

My enthusiasm for lower minimums on some exotic bets is not meant to suggest that the right pools to play are necessarily the ones with low minimums that allow you to buy dozens or hundreds of cheap combinations. Generally speaking, horseplayers already probably buy too many combinations in some exotic pools, especially the simpler ones such as exactas. In what seems almost a hangover from the WPS-only days, some players still focus only on "having" the winning combination, to the exclusion of how many times they had it or what their total return was relative to their investment.

A common example of this is the exacta player who never bets to win because he thinks the payoffs are too low. Instead of $5 or $10 win mutuels, he wants $50 or $100 exactas. If you run into him after a race and ask him how he did, he may crow that he "had" the $64 exacta, as if he had played only that winning combination and brilliantly selected what amounts to a 31-1 shot. In fact, he may well have made a $2 five-horse exacta box, which costs $40, to get that $64 return. Investing $40 and getting back $64 is exactly the same as what would have happened if he had bet his $40 to show on a horse who paid $3.20 for $2—a bet he would be mortified to admit having made.

There are much smarter ways to play exactas and every other bet, but don't quit your day job quite yet. Significant long-term profitability is not a realistic goal for the vast majority of horseplayers. Far too much handicapping literature suggests otherwise, that a careful application of the author's methods will result in a reliable primary or secondary income. Most bettors always have and always will lose money, regardless of whether they are making win and place bets or playing the superfecta and pick four. There are no mechanical winning systems or surefire investment plans.

Playing the races is not a means to a reliable profit, but an end in itself, a uniquely fascinating problem-solving exercise more akin to completing a challenging crossword puzzle than to laboring for an hourly wage. Of course, it's even better than a crossword puzzle when you add in the brave and beautiful horses, the thrill of the contest, and the many other charms of a day at the track. If you told me in advance that I would only break even for the next 12 months at the races, I would still play them for the sheer enjoyment of it, and I think most racegoers would too.

The fan who does not want to become a reclusive record-keeper or have his mortgage-paying ability determined by photo finishes can still try to put himself in the best possible position to improve his current returns and at least create the opportunity for an occasional exhilarating and high-priced triumph. One of the key points of this book is that most players do not even give themselves the chance for that triumph because they bet the exotics poorly.

Exotic betting has improved the crossword puzzle of handicapping horse races. Just as a crossword aficionado will feel prouder and more satisfied solving a difficult acrostic than filling in the obvious three-letter answers to the crossword in *TV Guide*, a horseplayer who hits a pick three or a superfecta will enjoy himself much more than one clutching a win ticket on an 8-5 favorite.

At first glance, exotic betting may seem to have made the puzzle harder, since there are so many more choices to be made. In many ways, though, these bets have made the puzzle more accessible by offering many more methods of solving it.

Remember that raft of gigantic payouts at the beginning of this chapter, stemming from Giacomo's unlikely victory at $102.60? Giacomo is a lovely animal and his connections are some of the nicest people in the sport, but I could never have picked him, liked him even a little, or bet him, even at 50-1. An analysis of how the race was run and subsequent events all suggest that his victory was a function of chaos. The race fell apart, the better horses all had a bad day, and Giacomo, who would have finished about sixth in a normal year, wound up wearing the roses. These things happen.

TENTH RACE
Churchill
MAY 7, 2005

$1\frac{1}{4}$ MILES. (1.59^{2}) 131ST RUNNING OF THE KENTUCKY DERBY. Grade I. Purse $2,000,000 FOR THREE–YEAR–OLDS WITH AN ENTRY FEE OF $25,000 EACH AND A STARTING FEE OF $25,000 EACH. Supplemental nominations may be made upon payment of $200,000 and in accordance with the rules set forth. All fees, including supplemental nominations, in excess of$900,000 in the aggregate shall be paid to the winner. Churchill Downs Incorporated shall guarantee a minimum gross purse of $2,000,000. The winner shall receive $1,240,000, second place $400,000, third $200,000, fourth $100,000 and fifth $60,000 from theGuaranteed Purse. Colts and Geldings 126 lbs.; Fillies 121 pounds. The owner of the winner shall receive a gold trophy. Closed with 372 nominations and one supplemental nomination: GREELEY'S GALAXY.

Value of Race: $2,399,600 Winner $1,639,600; second $400,000; third $200,000; fourth $100,000; fifth $60,000. Mutuel Pool $42,296,149.00 Exacta Pool $19,132,958.00 Trifecta Pool $22,189,155.00 Superfecta Pool $7,422,552.00

Last Raced	Horse	M/Eqt.	A.	Wt	PP	¼	½	¾	1	Str	Fin	Jockey	Odds $1
9Apr05 ^{6}SA^{4}	Giacomo	L	3	126	10	$18^{1/2}$	$18^{2 1/2}$	$18^{1 1/2}$	11^{hd}	$6^{1/2}$	$1^{1/2}$	Smith M E	50.30
16Apr05 ^{9}Kee^{3}	Closing Argument	L	3	126	18	5^{hd}	$6^{1/2}$	6^{hd}	4^{hd}	$1^{1/2}$	$2^{1/2}$	Velasquez C	71.60
16Apr05 ^{9}OP^{1}	Afleet Alex	L f	3	126	12	11^{hd}	$11^{2 1/2}$	$9^{1/2}$	$6^{1 1/2}$	2^{1}	$3^{2 1/2}$	Rose J	4.50
30Apr05 ^{11}CD^{1}	Don't Get Mad		3	126	17	19^{6}	$19^{3 1/2}$	$19^{3 1/2}$	10^{hd}	$7^{1/2}$	$4^{2 3/4}$	Baze T C	29.20
9Apr05 ^{6}SA^{1}	Buzzards Bay	L f	3	126	20	$10^{1/2}$	10^{hd}	$7^{1/2}$	$5^{1/2}$	5^{hd}	$5^{1/2}$	Guidry M	46.30
9Apr05 ^{6}SA^{3}	Wilko	L	3	126	14	$13^{1/2}$	14^{hd}	$16^{2 1/2}$	$13^{1 1/2}$	$10^{1/2}$	6no	Nakatani C S	21.70
9Apr05 ^{9}Aqu^{1}	Bellamy Road	L	3	126	16	$3^{1/2}$	5^{2}	5^{2}	2^{hd}	3^{hd}	$7^{3/4}$	Castellano J J	2.60
16Apr05 ^{9}OP^{3}	Andromeda's Hero	L	3	126	2	16^{hd}	15^{2}	13^{hd}	16^{2}	$14^{1 1/2}$	8no	Bejarano R	57.30
16Apr05 ^{9}OP^{2}	Flower Alley	L b	3	126	7	4^{hd}	3^{hd}	2^{hd}	$7^{1 1/2}$	8^{1}	9^{hd}	Chavez J F	41.30
2Apr05 ^{12}GP^{1}	High Fly	L	3	126	11	6^{1}	4^{1}	3^{hd}	1^{hd}	4^{1}	10^{nk}	Bailey J D	7.10
9Apr05 ^{7}Haw^{1}	Greeley's Galaxy	L	3	126	9	17^{1}	$16^{1/2}$	14^{hd}	8^{hd}	$12^{2 1/2}$	$11^{2 1/4}$	Desormeaux K J	21.00
23Apr05 ^{9}Kee^{1}	Coin Silver	L	3	126	5	$14^{1/2}$	12^{hd}	$12^{1 1/2}$	$9^{1/2}$	11^{1}	$12^{1 1/4}$	Valenzuela P A	38.60
16Apr05 ^{9}OP^{5}	Greater Good	L	3	126	8	20	20	20	$17^{1/2}$	$15^{1/2}$	$13^{3/4}$	McKee J	58.40
2Apr05 ^{12}GP^{2}	Noble Causeway	L	3	126	4	12^{2}	$13^{2 1/2}$	15^{hd}	12^{hd}	$13^{1/2}$	$14^{2 1/2}$	Stevens G L	12.30
16Apr05 ^{9}Kee^{4}	Sun King	L	3	126	3	$9^{1/2}$	9^{hd}	8^{hd}	$15^{1 1/2}$	16^{4}	15^{4}	Prado E S	15.70
16Apr05 ^{9}Kee^{6}	Spanish Chestnut		3	126	13	$1^{1/2}$	$1^{1 1/2}$	$1^{1 1/2}$	3^{hd}	9^{hd}	16^{7}	Bravo J	71.00
23Apr05 ^{9}Kee^{2}	Sort It Out	L	3	126	1	$15^{1/2}$	17^{hd}	17^{hd}	18^{4}	$17^{2 1/2}$	$17^{3 1/4}$	Blanc B	61.90
23Apr05 ^{9}Kee^{5}	Going Wild	L b	3	126	19	2^{1}	2^{1}	$4^{1/2}$	14^{hd}	$18^{5 1/2}$	$18^{3 1/2}$	Valdivia J Jr	59.50
16Apr05 ^{9}Kee^{1}	Bandini	L	3	126	15	7^{hd}	8^{2}	$11^{1 1/2}$	20	19^{3}	19^{12}	Velazquez J R	6.80
16Apr05 ^{9}Kee^{2}	High Limit	L	3	126	6	8^{2}	7^{hd}	$10^{3 1/2}$	19^{hd}	20	20	Dominguez R A	22.50

OFF AT 6:11 Start Good. Won driving. Track fast.

TIME :22^{1}, :45^{1}, 1:09^{2}, 1:35^{4}, 2:02^{3} (:22.28, :45.38, 1:09.59, 1:35.88, 2:02.75)

$2 Mutuel Prices:				
	10 – GIACOMO	102.60	45.80	19.80
	18 – CLOSING ARGUMENT		70.00	24.80
	12 – AFLEET ALEX			4.60

$2 EXACTA 10–18 PAID $9,814.80 $2 TRIFECTA 10–18–12 PAID $133,134.80
$1 SUPERFECTA 10–18–12–17 PAID $864,253.50

Gr/ro. c, (Feb), by Holy Bull – Set Them Free , by Stop the Music . Trainer Shirreffs John. Bred by Mr & Mrs J S Moss (Ky).

After the race, of course, plenty of people claimed Giacomo was an underappreciated overlay who deserved more respect and could have been picked by a clever and imaginative handicapper, but I do not believe that any rational path of analysis could have led to him as a selection or a win bet. It was the kind of completely crazy and unpredictable result that happens in roughly 1 out of every 100 races, and it just so happened that this "one" was the Kentucky Derby. (For the record, only two horses at 50-1 or better have triumphed in the 131-year history of the Derby.)

It is possible, however, that a very clever and imaginative exotics player could have stumbled into a piece of some of the monstrous payoffs he triggered. I find it far less likely that someone could have handicapped Giacomo to win the Derby than that someone might have viewed the race as having high chaos potential and made, say, a somewhat perverse seven-horse exacta box of the seven longest prices in the 20-horse field. That bet would have cost $42 at the $1 minimum and returned $4,907.40, half the posted $2 payout. That's a 115-1 return for a more plausible approach to the race than zeroing in on Giacomo to win at 50-1. Win bets on those same seven horses would have cost $14 and grossed $102.60, a return of less than 7-1.

Or maybe, just maybe, a well-heeled trifecta specialist enamored with the consistency of Afleet Alex (who finished third on an off day but subsequently proved himself by far the best of the bunch) could have keyed him to finish first, second, or third in the trifecta. Surrounding him with the entire field in this fashion would have cost $1,026. Keying him with 10 of his 19 opponents would have knocked the cost down to $270, and maybe those 10 would have included Giacomo and Closing Argument.

In the days before exotics, all you could do with the opinion that Afleet Alex would finish third or better, and that anything else was possible, was to bet him to show. Even with two massive longshots finishing in front of him, Afleet Alex paid only $4.60 to show, meaning a $270 show bet would have returned $621, and a $1,026 show bet would have grossed $2,359.80. Those are tidy little profits, but the $1 trifecta return for those two plays was quite a bit better—$66,567.40—while requiring a far more reasonable opinion than actually liking Giacomo to win the Kentucky Derby.

The remainder of this book provides a tour of exotic betting in American racing today. Chapter 2 is intended to be as painless as possible an introduction to the parimutuel mathematics and mechanics that govern the exotics. Chapter 3 introduces the intrarace exotic wagers—the exacta, trifecta, and superfecta—while Chapter 4 discusses the multirace varietals—the double, pick three, and pick four. Chapter 5 is a brief but necessary digression on your likely new partner in wagering, the Internal Revenue Service, while Chapter 6 is devoted to that unique creature (and object of my personal affection), the pick six.

Finally, Chapter 7 discusses one possible plan of attack for the recreational rather than professional horseplayers who devote less than every waking hour to the game: concentrating on the sport's big-event days, which frequently offer the very best exotic-betting opportunities of the year. It also recounts my own day at the races at the aforementioned 2005 Breeders' Cup, a day less remarkable for its chest-thumping successes than for its tantalizing opportunities—some of them fortuitously taken, others blockheadedly missed, but all of them available only in the new world of exotic wagering.

THE M*TH OF EXOTIC BETTING

THE BLEEPED LETTER in the chapter title above is nothing more exotic than an "a," withheld to avoid the general inclinations of readers, even horseplayers, to run away screaming from any discussion of mathematics. In the case of exotic wagering, however, it is a chat that can't be avoided.

You won't need a calculator to play along, and there will be no Greek letters or quadratic equations. It is a matter of basic arithmetic, and once you wrap your mind around it, the math of exotic betting is a compelling and nearly beautiful thing.

Let's begin by agreeing on what to call the different exotic bets and by taking a look at how they work and how payoffs are calculated.

The semantic classification of parimutuel bets varies from state to state, as well as internationally. An exacta in California is the same bet as an exactor in Canada or a perfecta at a Florida greyhound track. Nor is there agreement on what constitutes an exotic bet. Most often, WPS bets are called straight bets, two-horse bets are called multiple bets, and three-horse wagers such as trifectas and pick threes are exotics. In some jurisdictions, bets involving four or more horses are known as superexotics. For our purposes, every bet involving two or more horses is an exotic one.

Nearly all of the exotic bets fall into one of two categories: intrarace wagers, involving multiple finishers in the same race, or multirace wagers, bets that involve the winners of successive races. (The exception is the tiny category of hybrid wagers combining these, such as double quinellas and twin trifectas.) It may also help to think of these as either vertical or horizontal bets—the intrarace wagers running up and down the order of finish in one race, while the multirace winners stretch horizontally across two or more races.

The following chart summarizes how the major exotic wagers fall into these categories:

Horses	Intrarace (Vertical)	Multirace (Horizontal)
2	Exacta, Quinella	(Daily) Double
3	Trifecta	Pick Three
4	Superfecta	Pick Four
6	—	Pick Six

The other thing all the exotics have in common is that they are separate-pool wagers, meaning that they are not a part of, or derived from, the WPS pools. As we shall see, this is not merely a piece of racetrack-operation trivia, but one of the keys to the appeal of the exotic bets. To appreciate that, however, we must first examine how racetrack payouts are calculated and how much money the "house" keeps on different types of bets.

Takeout

One of the reasons that there is official and conflicting nomenclature for the various bet types is that words such as *multiple, exotic,* and *superexotic* are enshrined in the laws of the 37 different American states that permit parimutuel wagering. Racing's betting pools are taxed off the top by government and track operators, and different types of bets are subject to different rates of taxation.

In the 1930's and 1940's, a pre-lottery, pre-casino era when racing had a virtual monopoly on legal wagering, the takeout—the amount taken off the top of the pool before the remainder is paid out to those holding winning tickets—was only 10 percent. That figure was widely raised to 15 percent after World War II, held steady for over a generation, then began to creep up again in the 1970's and 1980's as track operators found themselves in competition with new state-sanctioned forms of gambling. They also managed to convince regulators that they should be allowed to extract a higher takeout rate on the new exotic wagers, arguing that horseplayers would neither notice nor feel the difference should they be lucky enough to hit one of these newfangled bonanzas.

The following chart shows the chaotic variety of takeout rates as of January 2006 in some of racing's major jurisdictions:

	Straight (1)	Multiple (2)	Exotic (3+)
California	15.43%	20.68%	20.68%
Florida	15.00%	20.00%	25.00%
Illinois	17.00%	20.50%	25.00%
Kentucky	16.00%	19.00%	19.00%
New York	14.00%	17.50%	25.00%
Pennsylvania	17.00%	20.00%	30.00%

These rates can change from year to year and even from track to track within the same state. In Florida, for example, Gulfstream Park uses the 15/20/25 rates listed above, while Calder has raced at 18/20/27 and Tampa Bay Downs at 18/21.5/25.9. In New York, maximums are set by statute, and operators can experiment with lower rates. There are nearly as many variations as there are states with parimutuel wagering, but there is one constant: Bets involving more than one horse are subjected to a larger takeout than WPS bets.

Takeout is necessary; without it, payoffs would be higher, but racetracks would have no funds for operations or to pay race purses, and government would receive no revenue. It is the takeout that effectively pays for the entire game. In 2005, Americans bet roughly $15 billion, and the total takeout was about $3 billion (a blended average of 20 percent combining all the differing rates). Roughly $1 billion of that was paid out in purses to horse owners, trainers, and jockeys, with the remaining $2 billion going to track operations and profits and statutory payments to state treasuries.

Takeout is much higher in racing than in most gambling propositions, the notable exception being state lotteries, where government takes as much as 50 percent off the top. But racing's takeout rates of between 15 and 25 percent compare very unfavorably with those in sports betting (4.54 percent), roulette (5.26 percent), and even slot machines (an average of 10 percent). This speaks not only to the high infrastructural costs of staging horse races, but also to the generally inefficient operation of racing and its declining share of the gambling market.

To understand the effect of takeout on payoffs, imagine that you and nine friends have gathered around a table to wager among yourselves on the result of a 10-horse race.

Each of you puts up $20 and picks a different horse. The backer of the winner will get the combined $200 sitting in the middle of the table. You could go so far as to say that every horse in the race is going off at 9-1 in your private little win pool, and the parimutuel win payoff will be $20—that is, $20 for every $2 bet, or $200 for $20.

But what if, before handing over the $200, the host of this little gathering announces that he is going take 15 percent out of the pool to pay for beverages and snacks? He removes $30 from the $200 in the middle of the table, a 15 percent takeout rate, leaving just $170 for the winner. We would now say that the winner got odds of only 7.5-1, and that his win payoff was $17 for $2, not $20 for $2.

Now imagine that your group is betting exactas instead of just picking winners. Assuming this gathering is being held in Florida, where the takeout rates are 15 percent on win bets and 20 percent on two-horse multiples, the host would take $40 rather than $30 out of the $200 pot, leaving just $160 rather than $170 for distribution to the winner. If you were betting trifectas or pick fours, the host would extract 25 percent rather than 15 or 20 percent, taking $50 out of the middle.

If this festive party goes on long enough, the guests will go broke, because takeout is not a one-time charge: It is applied on every race to an ever-diminishing collective guest bankroll. If the guests arrive with a combined $200 and the takeout is 20 percent, after one race the guests now have a combined $160 and the host has $40. They bet their remaining $160 on the next race and the host takes another $32, leaving them with $128, which is further reduced to $102.40 after the third race. After 10 races, the guests have just $21.48 left (an average of $2.15 apiece from their original $20), and the host has extracted $178.52 for what had better be gold-plated potato chips.

It is this giant hand reaching into the middle of the table in every single betting pool that makes racing such a difficult game to beat. Without takeout, anyone who was even a tiny bit better than the others at the table would make a long-term profit. With takeout, you must not only beat the other players, but also be sufficiently skilled to overcome the relentlessly grabbing giant hand.

Given the enormity of the takeout bite, why would anyone bet into pools other than the ones with the lowest possible takeout? Why would you play a superfecta at a 25 percent takeout instead of win bets at 15 percent?

Free (or Cheap) Odds

I was asked that question almost daily when I began gambling regularly in the press boxes of New York tracks as a cub reporter in the early 1980's. My wagering mentor was a retired writer and track executive named Pat Lynch, an astute and grizzled handicapper whose retirement package had included a front-row press-box seat for life from which to play the races. Lynch, who had been making his own speed figures decades before Beyer Speed Figures made their way into past performances, had spent a lifetime honing his numbers and his analytical skills to the point where he could show a small profit against the win-pool takeout, even as it had grown from 10 to 15 percent over the years.

Lynch would spend his mornings transcribing his figures into the *Daily Racing Form*'s past performances, and his afternoons waiting for the public to allow a logical horse to go off at a higher price than Lynch's figures said he should. He dismissed the few exotics permitted in New York at the time (one daily double, three exactas, and a last-race trifecta each day) as gimmicks, nothing but a ruse to raise the takeout on gullible players who were subjecting themselves to an impossibly high house advantage.

At first I was unable to justify to him why I was voluntarily playing in 20 or 25 percent takeout pools other than to say that I found them more fun, more challenging, and capable of producing the occasional large payout that his sober win bets never could. It was only later, when the pick six came to New York in 1985 and clobbered me over the head with the answer, that I was able to convince him that at least in theory, I was actually playing at a lower rate of takeout than he was.

The light bulb could have just as easily gone off at a grocery store. It's as simple as deciding which is the better buy—one apple for 15 cents, two apples for 20 cents, or three apples for 25 cents? By buying in bulk, you can reduce the cost per apple from 15 to 10 to 8 1/3 cents. Looked at slightly differently, once you buy the first apple for 15 cents, additional apples are only 5 cents apiece.

Of course, the volume discount is a bargain only if you actually want and will use more than one apple. Buying three for 25 cents and throwing away one or two means you're just paying 5 or 10 cents extra for that first apple, which is similar to what you are doing if you routinely wheel exactas or buy a 7-all-all trifecta instead of just betting the 7 to win. Sometimes such a bet might make sense—if, for example, you have an opinion that the favorites have a better than average chance of finishing out of the money and that there are plausible longshots who could round out the trifecta at big prices.

In that case, you truly want more than the first apple. You

are betting on three different things—on the 7 to win the race, on the possibility of a longshot finishing second, and the possibility of another longshot finishing third. The idea of incremental cost per apple is in play. You're paying 15 percent takeout on the first opinion but only 5 percent takeout on the second and third bets.

In every exotic wager, from the simple and familiar daily double to the most complex array of pick-six tickets, *you are making more than one bet at once.* This may sound stupefyingly obvious, but understanding that idea and its implications is itself a key to successful exotic play.

Let's stop comparing apples to mutuels and see how this actually works. The oldest and simplest exotic, the daily double, provides the clearest illustration.

The daily double, which used to be the only exotic wager on most racecards, requires that you select the winners of two races in advance. Potential payoffs for each winning double combination are posted during the betting before the first race.

The double, like all exotics, is a separate pool from the WPS pools on the two races, and horses might not be bet precisely the same way in both pools, but for the sake of this example, let's say that they are. Let's also say that the double consists of two five-horse fields and that you like one and only one horse in each race—a 4-1 shot in the opener and the 3-5 favorite in the second race—and let's say you're a genius and they both win.

What was the optimal way to bet them both to win their races—at a 15 percent takeout in the two win pools, or at a 20 percent takeout in the daily double?

First let's make sure we know how the win pool works. The first table below illustrates our hypothetical first race of the day, a five-horse field with a win pool of exactly $100,000:

WIN POOL—RACE 1				
Horse	**$ Bet**	**% of Pool**	**Odds**	**$2 Payoff**
1	$42,500	42.50%	1-1	$4.00
2	$28,333	28.33%	2-1	$6.00
3	$17,000	17.00%	4-1	$10.00
4	$ 8,500	8.50%	9-1	$20.00
5	$ 3,667	3.67%	22-1	$46.00

Total $100,000

Takeout -15,000

Payout $ 85,000

Notice that number 1 is even money and will return $4 for a $2 win bet. We think of such a horse as being "50-50" to win the race and might assume that 50 percent of the money has been bet on him. In fact, though, the horse has only 42.5 percent of the money in the pool. If there were no 15 percent win-pool takeout, there would be an extra $15,000 to pay off those who bet on the 1, and his $2 win payoff would be $4.70 rather than $4.

Similarly, the horse we like, number 3, is 4-1, meaning you will quintuple your money if he wins, getting a $10 win mutuel for a $2 bet. This would imply that he has attracted one-fifth of the pool, but in fact he has attracted only 17 percent of the money, not 20 percent, the difference again being due to the takeout.

Now let's look at the second race, where one horse has in fact attracted exactly 50 percent of the money in the win pool.

Here we see how takeout knocks a $4 mutuel down to $3.40, or what would otherwise be a 100 percent profit to a 70 percent profit. Because there is only $85,000, rather than $100,000, to pay off the $50,000 in winning bets, the favorite with half the pool on him will pay $3.40 rather than $4 to win.

WIN POOL—RACE 2				
Horse	$ Bet	% of Pool	Odds	$2 Payoff
1	$50,000	50.00%	7-10	$3.40
2	$28,333	28.33%	2-1	$6.00
3	$13,000	13.00%	5-1	$12.00
4	$ 5,000	5.00%	16-1	$34.00
5	$ 3,667	3.67%	22-1	$46.00

Total $100,000

Takeout -15,000

Payout $ 85,000

A daily double of these two races is an entirely separate pool, but we are assuming that the horses are supported in exactly the same proportions in the double pool as they are to win—that, for example, 42.5 percent of all the double tickets sold have number 1 in the first race and 50 percent of all the tickets sold have number 1 in the second race. We multiply 42.5 percent by 50 percent to find that 21.25 percent of all the daily-double tickets sold are on the 1-1 combination, which will therefore pay $7.40 if it comes in, after the 20 percent takeout on daily-double bets. (It should be $7.53, but thanks to the additional takeout of breakage—the practice of rounding down payoffs to the nearest 10- or 20-cent increment—it will actually return $7.50 in New York or Canada and $7.40 elsewhere in the United States.)

With two five-horse fields, there are 25 different daily-double combinations. We can apply this same multiplication of percentages from the win pool and see how each of the 25 double combinations might be bet in a hypothetical $100,000 double pool.

DD	% Race 1	% Race 2	% DD Pool	$DD Pool	$2 DD Pays
1-1	42.50%	50.00%	21.25%	$21,250	$ 7.40
1-2	42.50%	28.33%	12.04%	$12,041	$ 13.20
1-3	42.50%	13.00%	5.52%	$ 5,525	$ 28.80
1-4	42.50%	5.00%	2.12%	$ 2,125	$ 75.20
1-5	42.50%	3.67%	1.55%	$ 1,558	$ 102.60
2-1	28.33%	50.00%	14.16%	$14,167	$ 11.20
2-2	28.33%	28.33%	8.02%	$ 8,028	$ 19.80
2-3	28.33%	13.00%	3.68%	$ 3,683	$ 43.40
2-4	28.33%	5.00%	1.41%	$ 1,417	$ 112.80
2-5	28.33%	3.67%	1.03%	$ 1,039	$ 154.00
3-1	17.00%	50.00%	8.50%	$ 8,500	$ 18.80
3-2	17.00%	28.33%	4.81%	$ 4,817	$ 33.20
3-3	17.00%	13.00%	2.21%	$ 2,210	$ 72.40
3-4	17.00%	5.00%	0.85%	$ 850	$ 188.20
3-5	17.00%	3.67%	0.62%	$ 623	$ 256.60
4-1	8.50%	50.00%	4.25%	$ 4,250	$ 37.60
4-2	8.50%	28.33%	2.40%	$ 2,408	$ 66.40
4-3	8.50%	13.00%	1.11%	$ 1,105	$ 144.80
4-4	8.50%	5.00%	0.43%	$ 425	$ 376.40
4-5	8.50%	3.67%	0.31%	$ 312	$ 513.20
5-1	3.67%	50.00%	1.83%	$ 1,834	$ 87.20
5-2	3.67%	28.33%	1.04%	$ 1,039	$ 154.00
5-3	3.67%	13.00%	0.48%	$ 476	$ 335.60
5-4	3.67%	5.00%	0.18%	$ 183	$ 872.60
5-5	3.67%	3.67%	0.13%	$ 134	$1,189.80
Total			100.00%	$100,000	

Total $100,000
Takeout -20,000
Payout $ 80,000

There are 25 possible combinations over which the $100,000 is spread, almost as if it were a 25-horse race with starters going off as low as 5-2 (the combination of the two favorites) and as high as 593-1 (the double combining the two 22-1 outsiders). Every exotic pool works this way, with many, many more possible combinations as the exoticness increases: A similar chart for four 10-horse fields in a pick four would require 10,000 rather than 25 lines.

For the moment, though, let's return to the question of what was the best way to bet our fancied 3 in the first race and the 1 in the second race.

If we bet $2 to win on number 3 at 4-1 in the first, we would get back $10. If we then bet that $10 back on the 1 at 7-10 in the second, we would get back $17. But if we bet a double of 3 and 1, we should get back $18.80, a return that is over 10 percent better than the $17 parlay of the two winners.

How can this be, given that the takeout in the double is 20 percent as opposed to a rate of only 15 percent on the win bets? The answer is that we are making two bets but being subjected to the takeout once rather than twice, so we are getting the second wager, or apple, at a discount.

Here is another way of saying the same thing. At a 20 percent rather than 15 percent win-pool takeout, our first-race winner would pay $9.40 rather than $10 to win. But then in the second race, where only 50 percent of the betting is on the 7-10 favorite, we get the full value of his accounting for only half of the betting. The $9.40 is doubled to $18.80, instead of the $10 returning just $17 after a second dose of 15 percent takeout. We have gotten nearly "free" odds on the favorite in the second—the full double-your-money value of a horse who has attracted 50 percent of the betting, rather than the difference between $3.40 and $4 caused by takeout.

No one is going to retire on that $1.80 difference, but improving your return by over 10 percent is worth a lot more in the long term. For a good handicapper who is currently outwitting the crowd and getting back a 95 percent return, a 10 percent swing brings him to 105 percent, meaning a 5 percent profit rather than a 5 percent loss. And it gets better: Increasingly complex wagers compound this advantage to produce much better than a 10 percent bonus.

It is important to remember, however, that in this example we had two correct winning opinions. The point is that an exotic wager is an inherently better way to leverage two or more such opinions when they are correct and you are receiving fair or advantageous odds, not that every two-horse bet is inherently better than every one-horse bet, or that a two-horse bet is necessarily a better way to bet a single horse. Simply turning a win bet into a double or an exacta with no attempt to incorporate an advantageous second opinion into the equation is only doing what Pat Lynch said exotic betting would—making a win bet at a higher rate of takeout.

Let's stick with the previous example and table to see how this works. Suppose that we still like the 3 at 4-1 in the first race, but we are absolutely clueless about the second race of the day. Every horse seems to be the correct price and we have no preferences whatsoever. If we played doubles with number 3 in the first to everyone in the second—a $2 double "wheel"—we would spend $10 on five $2 double combinations and get one of the following sums back for our $10 investment, depending on who wins the second race: $18.80, $33.20, $72.40, $188.20, or $256.60.

Betting $10 to win would have gotten a $50 return. This way, we get substantially less if one of the two favorites wins the second, and more if one of the three outsiders does. All we are effectively doing is making a same-sized win bet on every single horse in the second race. We might as well play roulette. We are throwing away the 4-1 value of our opinion in the first if either of the two most likely outcomes occurs in the second. It is lunacy, but many horseplayers gamble this way.

What if, instead, we attempted to equalize our return by betting more on the shorter-priced double combinations and less on the longshots in the second? To make it come out with close to an equal return for every outcome, we need to use more hypothetical money since you can't make win bets in increments of less than a dollar. Here is how it might work:

Combo	$2 Payoff	Bet	Return
3-1	$ 18.80	$110	$1,034
3-2	$ 33.20	$ 62	$1,029
3-3	$ 72.40	$ 29	$1,049
3-4	$188.20	$ 11	$1,035
3-5	$256.60	$ 8	$1,026
Total bet		$220	

You would bet a total of $220 to get back returns of between $1,026 and $1,049—all of them less than the $1,100 you would get for betting the $220 to win at 4-1. All you have accomplished with this "weighted" wheel is to subject yourself to the higher rate of takeout by playing the double at 20 percent instead of a win bet at 15 percent.

What's missing is that crucial second opinion. It doesn't even have to be a radical one or particularly clever. Let's say that instead of being smart enough to declare the second-race favorite a cinch, you have an apparently unimpressive opinion that either the 7-10 favorite or the 2-1 second choice will win the race. Try as you might, you can't make a plausible case for the other three, who you think can only win by default in the unlikely event that both of the favorites misfire. The win bettors have effectively said it is 78.3 percent likely that either number 1 (50 percent of the pool) or number 2 (28.33 percent of the pool) will win, but you think it's more like 95 percent and are willing to gamble that at least one of them will show up and run his race.

Saying that you like the 7-10 shot and the 2-1 second choice may make your track buddies call you a chalk-eating coward with no real opinion, but it turns out to be a useful bit of leverage. To get the same return if either of them wins, you need about seven tickets on each of the $18.80 combos and four on each of the $33.20 payoffs. You might make a bet like this:

Combo	$2 Payoff	Bet	Return
3-1	$ 18.80	$140	$1,316
3-2	$ 33.20	$ 80	$1,328
Total bet		$ 220	

Now for the same $220 that got you between $1,026 and $1,049 with a weighted wheel, you are doing over 25 percent better with a return of either $1,316 or $1,328. This is also significantly better than the $1,100 you would get from a $220 win bet on the winner of the first race alone. Yes, you have introduced the risk of getting nothing if one of the three long-shots wins the second, but if you honestly believe there is only a 5 percent chance that will happen, you will do well in the long run by assuming that additional risk. Look what happens if you do it 100 times each way. Collecting an average of $1,039 100 percent of the time gets you back $103,900. Getting back an average of $1,322 95 percent of the time gets you $125,661—still 15 percent better than the weighted wheel, even with the introduction of risk and a 5 percent wipeout rate.

If you could only make WPS bets, you probably wouldn't touch the second race with a 10-foot pole. Your perception that the 1 or the 2 winning the race is a 95 percent rather than 78 percent probability barely covers the 15 percent takeout in the win pools. To bet them both to win would require you to bet $100 at 7-10 on number 1 and $57 to win on number 2 at 2-1, a total investment of $157 to get back either $170 or $171 95 percent of the time and to wipe out 5 percent of the time. However, by using the daily-double pool, you are able to get nearly the full value of that discrepancy and magnify the value of your opinion on the winner of the first race.

Capitalizing on Public Error

The previous examples show how exotic betting can be rewarding by allowing you to combine two or more opinions to receive effectively lower takeout or higher odds. But this tells only part of the story of why exotics can be so productive. For the sake of clarity, these examples all made the assumption that the exotic pools directly mirrored the win odds. While they generally do in the broadest sense, there are frequent deviations that create an additional reservoir of opportunity.

These deviations come in two forms: handicapping mistakes and betting mistakes. Either type creates situations where some exotic combinations are underlaid, meaning that their odds are too low relative to their actual likelihood of happening, and others are overlaid, meaning that their odds are very generous relative to their true chances.

Finding underlays and overlays is the foundation of any success at parimutuel wagering, simple or exotic. A horse with a true 50-50 chance of winning a race is a terrible bet at 2-5 and a great bet at 2-1. Think of it in terms of betting $2 on coin flips. If you're losing $2 when you're wrong and winning 80 cents when you're right, you're going to go broke very quickly. If you're losing $2 when you're wrong and winning $4 when you're right, you will eventually become a millionaire.

Unfortunately, racing is not that easy, and the public at large is not entirely dim. Of course we can all recall instances where we thought a 10-1 shot should have been 2-1 or a 2-5 shot was a throwout, but in general the public gets it basically right in the win pool. Their top choice wins a third of the time, year in and year out, a better record than any individual handicapper can match making selections in every race. Their second choice wins more often than their third choice, which wins more often than their fourth choice.

It is a phenomenon that correlates directly to the thesis of the excellent 2003 book *The Wisdom of Crowds,* by the writer and economist James Surowiecki. He found, for example, that on the game show *Who Wants to be a Millionaire?*, the consensus answer of 100 tourists in the studio audience consistently was correct more often than the answer provided by any individual expert with a monstrous IQ and a wall full of graduate degrees. Translate that to thousands of bettors participating in the win pool, and the results are similar.

There were only four multiple-choice answers to each *Millionaire* question, and from six to 12 correct "answers" in a typical win pool, but the possibilities are more exotic in multiple-horse wagers. As we noted in Chapter 1, the same race that offers only eight possible win bets offers 56 possible exacta outcomes, 336 trifecta outcomes, and 1,680 superfecta permutations. The same public that is pretty good at ranking eight horses in declining order of likelihood of victory is not going to be as precise with 56 or 1,680 choices.

In large part, those choices correspond to the win pool, and the trifecta of the three favorites is of course always going to pay much less than one involving the three longest shots in the field. There is a great deal of room for chaos in between those extremes, however, and as mentioned above, these can be either handicapping or betting errors.

Here is an example of a handicapping error: The second choice in the win pool, a horse who may legitimately be the second most likely winner of the race, is not necessarily the second most likely second-place finisher. Perhaps he is a speed-crazed front-runner who becomes brave when left alone to set a leisurely pace but crumbles if he is challenged early. He will, however, probably be bet in the exacta pool as the second most likely horse to finish second, making the exactas with him finishing second underlays while inflating the prices on other combinations.

A betting error does not necessarily involve a bad opinion about a horse by the public, but rather reflects poor mechanics in their actual wagering, frequently as a function of ingrained bad habits or bankroll limitations. Pick threes involving victories by three consecutive second choices, for example, may pay less than the win-pool odds on such horses might suggest simply because so many players make a 2 x 2 x 2 part-wheel. Another frequent betting error is that trifecta overlays often occur when a longshot finishes second because so many trifecta players construct their tickets using longshots only in the bottom position.

Both kinds of errors—opinion-based handicapping errors and mechanically based betting errors—create an inefficiency, and thus an opportunity for the exotic bettor.

The Place and Show Fallacy

This section may seem slightly out of order, since we dismissed place and show betting in a single breath in Chapter 1 and are well into the discussion of the potential for improving on win odds through exotic wagering. Some readers, however, are probably still wondering why place and show aren't perfectly good alternatives to betting a horse to finish second in an exacta or third in a trifecta, given the lower takeout in the WPS pools.

Now that we have seen how win and daily-double pools are calculated, however, it is probably time to look at how place and show pools actually work and why they are rarely wise choices.

Let's return to our Race 1 example from above, and again let's assume that the horses are being bet in the same proportions in the $50,000 place pool as they are in the $100,000 win pool.

Horse	$ Win	% of Pool	$ Place	Win Odds
1	$42,500	42.50%	$21,250	1-1
2	$28,333	28.33%	$14,167	2-1
3	$17,000	17.00%	$ 8,500	4-1
4	$ 8,500	8.50%	$ 4,250	9-1
5	$ 3,667	3.67%	$ 1,833	22-1
Total	$100,000		$50,000	
Takeout	-15,000		-7,500	
Payout	$ 85,000		$42,500	

In the place pool, two different sets of ticket holders are paid—both those who bet to place on the winner and those who bet to place on the second-place finisher.

Again let's say that our fancied 4-1 shot won the race, and let's say that the even-money favorite finished second. Our horse's win price was a simple calculation: Subtract the 15 percent takeout from $100,000, leaving $85,000 to be paid to the holders of $17,000 in win tickets, or $5 for every $1, creating an official payoff of $10 for $2.

The place pool has a few more steps and wrinkles to it:

1. Subtract the takeout. Since 15 percent of $50,000 is $7,500, that leaves $42,500 to be paid out.
2. Pay every bettor back his $2. This is done first in order to ensure that there is enough money to cover all the winning bets. So we subtract the $21,250 bet on number 1 and the $8,500 bet on number 3, a total of $29,750. Subtract $29,750 from the payout pool of $42,500, which leaves $12,750 in profits to be paid out.
3. Divide that $12,750 in half, giving $6,375 to each group of ticket holders.
4. Calculate the place payoff for number 3, who finished first: Those who backed him to place will receive $6,375 in profit on their $8,500 in winning place bets, which works out to 73.5 cents on the dollar or $1.47 on each $2. So number 3 should pay $3.47 to place, which is knocked down by breakage to $3.40.
5. Calculate the place payoff for number 1, who finished second: Those who backed him to place will receive $6,375 in profit on their $21,500 in winning place bets, which works out to 30 cents on the dollar or 60 cents on each $2 bet. So number 1 will pay $2.60 to place.

The first two lines of WPS payoffs on the race now look like this:

Horse	Win	Place
3 Our Hero	$10.00	$3.40
1 The Favorite		$2.60

So Our Hero, who quintupled our money paying $10 for $2 to win, doesn't even double our money to place, returning a 70 percent profit instead of a 400 percent profit. Sure, sometimes Our Hero will finish second and we'll at least get something back, but he would have to finish second nearly three times as often as he wins to produce the same return. The same is true for The Favorite—you're getting a 30 rather than 100 percent profit with a $2.60 place payoff instead of a $4 win payoff.

This example shows the two biggest problems with place betting. The first is that you are completely at the mercy of which horse will be the other participant in the place pool. In this case, the second-place finish by the heavy favorite means that a great deal of the pool is eaten up paying off his backers, leaving relatively little to split in the way of profits.

The other problem is the breakage issue. In this example, for clarity's sake we used round numbers that produced a payoff of precisely $2.60 for The Favorite with a 15 percent takeout and single breakage, the prevailing rules in New York. But look what happens if we move this pool to Kentucky, where the takeout is just one point higher at 16 percent and payoffs are rounded down to the nearest 20-cent rather than 10-cent increment. With $42,000 rather than $42,500 to pay off the winning place bets, a seemingly insignificant difference of only $500, the place payoff on The

Favorite goes down from precisely $2.60 to $2.57, which is then rounded all the way down to $2.40. Getting $2.40 when you should be getting $2.57 is a 30 percent reduction in the profit you deserve, an insurmountable additional tax to pay on a regular basis.

Show betting compounds the problem because now there is a third group of ticket holders that need to have their initial bets returned and then take a third of the profit pool. Without belaboring the math, here are the show payoffs if Our Hero and the two favorites run 1-2-3:

Horse	Win	Place	Show
3 Our Hero	$10.00	$3.40	$2.30
1 The Favorite		$2.60	$2.10
2 Second Choice			$2.20

Obviously, the place payoffs will be higher if the favorite runs worse than second and the show payoffs will be better if the favorite runs worse than third. If our 4-1 shot wins and the 2-1 second choice finishes second, their respective place payoffs will be $4.20 and $3.40 rather than the $3.40 and $2.60 above. In the unlikely event that both favorites finish worse than second and the 9-1 shot is the runner-up, the place payoff on Our Hero will increase from $3.40 to $5.40. But even in this unusual case, you're only getting a profit of just $3.40 to place as opposed to an $8 profit on a win bet.

Here's the even more important point about that situation: Let's say that you had good reason to think there was a greater likelihood of both those favorites running poorly than their odds would suggest. Or maybe you actually liked that 9-1 shot and thought he had a better than 9-1 chance of running second. Making a place bet on Our Hero to get a $5.40 payoff if that happens is an extremely inefficient way to capitalize on your perception. Which would you rather do—increase your $3.40 place payoff to $5.40, or improve your $10 win payoff to the $90 exacta payoff that should occur when a 4-1 beats a 9-1?

Assuming you chose the latter, it's clearly time to leave the dreary and unrewarding world of place and show wagering for the greener pastures of multihorse, intrarace bets.

3 INTRARACE EXOTICS

ALTHOUGH THE daily double introduced bettors to multirace betting decades before exactas and trifectas became commonplace, the one-race or intrarace exotics are the most popular wagers in American racing today. In the wagering on the eight Breeders' Cup races in 2005, for example, the breakdown was as follows:

Intrarace	$ 57,141,735	51.0 %
Straight	$ 38,763,082	34.6 %
Multirace	$ 16,102,647	14.4 %
TOTAL	$112,007,464	100.0%

That $57.1 million had three components: The eight exactas handled $26.2 million, the eight trifectas attracted $22.7 million, and the eight superfectas accounted for the remaining $8.2 million. This generally reflects the current popularity of the three intrarace wagers and corresponds to both their longevity and their difficulty.

Exactas are the oldest, cheapest, and simplest of the trio, while the more recent trifectas have been catching up each year. Superfectas, only introduced to the Breeders' Cup in 1998, are attracting a growing percentage of the intrarace handle each year but are still a distant third. Dime superfectas, though still unavailable on the Triple Crown and Breeders' Cup races, may narrow that annual gap.

All these bets are popular for the same basic reason: The posted payoffs are always higher than on a win bet alone, making the player feel as if he has accomplished a more difficult and rewarding task. Even players who now focus on these wagers for better and more sophisticated reasons probably began with that motive of sheer greed. Who wants a $4.60 or $9.20 win payoff when there are $100 exactas and $1,000 trifectas out there for the taking?

What makes the intrarace bets even more seductive is that they can simultaneously seem not only more rewarding but also easier than picking a winner. If you can't choose among three contenders you like, it may seem as though you have a greater chance of cashing a ticket by boxing all three of them in an exacta than by choosing one of the three to win. For many people, a bet such as the exacta provides a way to get some betting action without having a real opinion.

Those are the people whose money you should be trying to take in the exotic pools. There are times you will be playing exotics without a strong win preference and times when you will be casting a wide net, but not out of indecision or desperation. As discussed in the previous chapter, the foundation of successful exotic betting is having two or more advantageous opinions, not zero opinions.

Combinations and Costs

The progression from exacta to trifecta to superfecta is in one sense simply a matter of burrowing deeper and deeper into the order of finish in a race, from 1-2 to 1-2-3 to 1-2-3-4. With each additional finisher included, both the cost and the difficulty increase. For many players, the choice of pool selection is entirely a function of whether their bankroll can accommodate what they consider a comfortable amount of coverage in a race.

Let's use our hypothetical five-horse field to see how each bet has a different number of possible combinations. In a five-horse field, there are limited ways that numbers 1 through 5 can finish first and second in the race:

1-2	1-3	1-4	1-5
2-1	2-3	2-4	2-5
3-1	3-2	3-4	3-5
4-1	4-2	4-3	4-5
5-1	5-2	5-3	5-4

Note that when we looked at how a daily double works in the previous chapter, there were 25 combinations with a pair of five-horse races, but now there are only 20 exacta combinations in a five-horse field. Why isn't it 5 x 5 in both cases? The difference is that while number 3 can win both the first race and the second race to produce a 3-3 daily double, number 3 cannot finish both first and second in a single race, so there is no such thing as a 1-1, 2-2, 3-3, 4-4, or 5-5 exacta.

This might seem so obvious that your cocker spaniel should understand it, but this underlying point is a key factor in why people often miscalculate both the cost and likely payoffs of intrarace exotics.

When we move on to the trifecta, the number of possible combinations increases from 20 to 60 in a five-horse field. For each of the 20 exacta combinations listed above, there are three possible trifectas. A 1-2 exacta can continue on to become either a 1-2-3, 1-2-4, or 1-2-5 trifecta, depending on who finishes third. Here are all 60 possible trifecta outcomes in a five-horse field:

1-2-3	1-2-4	1-2-5	1-3-2	1-3-4	1-3-5
1-4-2	1-4-3	1-4-5	1-5-2	1-5-3	1-5-4
2-1-3	2-1-4	2-1-5	2-3-1	2-3-4	2-3-5
2-4-1	2-4-3	2-4-5	2-5-1	2-5-3	2-5-4
3-1-2	3-1-4	3-1-5	3-2-1	3-2-4	3-2-5
3-4-1	3-4-2	3-4-5	3-5-1	3-5-2	3-5-4
4-1-2	4-1-3	4-1-5	4-2-1	4-2-3	4-2-5
4-3-1	4-3-2	4-3-5	4-5-1	4-5-2	4-5-3
5-1-2	5-1-3	5-1-4	5-2-1	5-2-3	5-2-4
5-3-1	5-3-2	5-3-4	5-4-1	5-4-2	5-4-3

The superfecta increases the possibilities again, usually more so than in this example of a five-horse field. (Most tracks don't even permit superfecta wagering on fields this small.) In this instance, there are only two superfecta combinations for each trifecta combination because there are only two more horses in the race to fill out the fourth position. So, for example, we go only from 12 possible trifectas to 24 possible superfecta combinations when number 1 finishes first:

1-2-3-4	1-2-3-5	1-2-4-3	1-2-4-5	1-2-5-3	1-2-5-4
1-3-2-4	1-3-2-5	1-3-4-2	1-3-4-5	1-3-5-2	1-3-5-4
1-4-2-3	1-4-2-5	1-4-3-2	1-4-3-5	1-4-5-2	1-4-5-3
1-5-2-3	1-5-2-4	1-5-3-2	1-5-3-4	1-5-4-2	1-5-4-3

There are 24 similar possibilities for each of the other four potential winners, for a total of 120 possible combinations.

In a five-horse field, then, there are 20 possible exactas, 60 possible trifectas, and 120 possible superfectas. This is not a constant ratio, as the following chart of possible combinations in different field sizes shows:

Field	Ex	Tri	Super
3	6	6	—
4	12	24	24
5	20	60	120
6	30	120	360
7	42	210	840
8	56	336	1,680
9	72	504	3,024
10	90	720	5,040
11	110	990	7,920
12	132	1,320	11,880
13	156	1,716	17,160
14	182	2,184	24,024
20	380	6,840	116,280

Let's make sure we understand how to arrive at the numbers in this chart. As noted above, there are 20 rather than 25 exacta combinations in a five-horse field because the formula is 5 x 4 and not 5 x 5, since there are no 1-1 or 4-4 exacta combinations. In the trifecta, there are not only no 1-1-1 combinations, but also no 1-1-2 or 1-2-1 combinations. So we say that a five-horse $1 trifecta box costs $60 by multiplying not 5 x 5 x 5, but 5 x 4 x 3. With each additional finisher, we subtract 1 from each position to reflect the impossibility of multiple placings by the same horse. So in an eight-horse race, there are not 8 x 8 x 8 possible trifectas, but 8 x 7 x 6, or 336. The superfecta in that race has 8 x 7 x 6 x 5, or 1,680, possible combinations.

This chart can also be used to calculate the cost of "boxing" the number of horses in the first column with $1 bets. Boxing means purchasing all the possible permutations of a selected number of horses on a single ticket. This allows you to call out or punch in a three-horse "box" of 1-5-7 instead of delineating all six of the individual combinations (1-5, 1-7, 5-1, 5-7, 7-1, 7-5). Just as there are 20 possible exacta combinations in a five-horse field, there are 20 possible combinations when you box any five horses in a field of any size.

Boxing horses in exactas is appealing because of its convenience. It's a good thing for newcomers or elderly relatives to do because it is inexpensive (as little as $6 for a three-horse $1 box) and easy to explain. If any two of the horses in your box run first and second, you win and you get a payoff that looks a lot better than the win-pool mutuel. By your second, or 20th or 200th visit to the track, however, you should begin to see that three-horse boxes usually provide a very poor return and that their apparent convenience is an invitation to highly inefficient betting.

The first problem with boxing three or more horses is that you are making a large number of individual bets, perhaps more than you really want to make and frequently more than justify your likely return. If you make a $2 five-horse exacta box and you hit the winning $56 combination, you will feel elated only until you realize that you invested $40 and got back $56, the equivalent of a $2.80 place or show payoff. It's also easy to win but lose in such a situation. A "winning" five-horse box with a $32 payoff actually means you bet $40 and got back $32—that is, you lost $8.

The next problem with boxing is that you are agreeing to bet the same amount on each of the 6 or 12 or 20 or 56 combinations you are boxing. Do you really want to have every one of them in equal strength? Wouldn't it probably make more sense to have some of them for only $1 but others for more? What having a simple box does is reduce you to hoping for the longest-priced and frequently least-likely combination. You're probably rooting against your better judgment and you're back to throwing dice or playing roulette. Just saying "these are my four horses" isn't really an opinion, much less two or more good opinions.

Boxing is almost as bad as wheeling, which we discussed relative to the daily double in Chapter 2. A simple wheel—keying your horse over the entire field in equal strength—is sheer gambling, and a weighted wheel, where you bet more on the short-priced combinations and less on the longer ones, is just an elaborate win bet at a higher rate of takeout.

A partial wheel, or "part-wheel," is a slight improvement. We're approaching intelligent exotic-betting territory now, because you are combining two opinions—that the horse you are part-wheeling is a worthy key, and that you believe only a limited number of the opposition can finish second. Just be careful that by "limited," you're not using too many horses, or all of the favorites, so that you're not really improving on making a win bet.

Let's go back to our recurring five-horse-race example,

where you like number 3, Our Hero, at 4-1. Let's say that the four exactas with him on top—probable exacta payoffs are posted throughout the betting before a race—are paying the following for a $2 bet:

3-1	$ 18
3-2	$ 27
3-4	$ 90
3-5	$200

If all you do is discard the hapless longshot, number 5, and make three exactas—3-1, 3-2, and 3-4—you will invest $6 for a return of either $18, $27, or $90. This works out well if the 4 runs second at 9-1, but otherwise you would have done better by betting that $6 to win for a $30 return. If you really think number 4 has a reasonably good chance at running second, it might be wiser to focus on that combination in the exacta while making a win bet and/or keying number 3 in a multirace bet such as a double or pick three.

There is no point in making an exacta, or any other exotic bet, unless you have that additional opinion. Otherwise you are just diluting your win price and trying to get lucky. The whole idea here is to get an even better price than is available in the win pool.

Did those possible payoffs above seem skimpy? When we looked at this race as the first half of a hypothetical daily double in Chapter 2, we said that a double involving number 3 at 4-1 with a 2-1 shot in the second race should pay $33.20. So why should an exacta of a 4-1 shot over a 2-1 shot pay only $27?

Intrarace payoffs

Here is the exacta equivalent of the daily-double chart from page 33, showing the exacta payoffs in our five-horse race if the horses are bet in the same proportions they are in the win pool:

EXACTA POOL

(Takeout: 15% WPS, 20% Exacta; Breakage: NY rules)

Win odds: #1: 1-1; #2: 2-1; #3: 4-1; #4: 9-1; #5: 22-1

Exacta	1st/2nd Win Odds	%Pool	$2 Exacta Pays
1-2	1-1/2-1	20.94%	$ 7.60
1-3	1-1/4-1	12.56%	$ 12.60
1-4	1-1/9-1	6.28%	$ 25.40
1-5	1-1/22-1	2.71%	$ 59.00
Subtotal		42.50%	
2-1	2-1/1-1	16.80%	$ 9.50
2-3	2-1/4-1	6.72%	$ 23.80
2-4	2-1/9-1	3.36%	$ 47.60
2-5	2-1/22-1	1.45%	$110.00
Subtotal		28.33%	
3-1	4-1/1-1	8.71%	$ 18.20
3-2	4-1/2-1	5.80%	$ 27.40
3-4	4-1/9-1	1.74%	$ 91.50
3-5	4-1/22-1	0.75%	$213.00
Subtotal		17.00%	

Exacta	1st/2nd Win Odds	%Pool	$2 Exacta Pays
4-1	9-1/1-1	3.95%	$ 40.40
4-2	9-1/2-1	2.63%	$ 60.50
4-3	9-1/4-1	1.58%	$101.00
4-5	9-1/22-1	0.34%	$469.00
Subtotal		8.50%	
5-1	22-1/1-1	1.62%	$ 98.50
5-2	22-1/2-1	1.08%	$148.00
5-3	22-1/4-1	0.65%	$247.00
5-4	22-1/9-1	0.32%	$494.50
Subtotal		3.67%	
GRAND TOTAL		100.00%	

When you first started going to the racetrack, somebody probably gave you a formula for what an exacta "should" pay—possibly the win price multiplied by the runner-up's place price or, more commonly, the win price times the runner-up's odds. What, for example, should happen when an even-money shot beats a 22-1 shot? As you're sitting there waiting for the result to be official, you might try to reason it out by saying that the winner is paying $4 for $2 and the runner-up should multiply that by 22 for an $88 payoff. Or you might think that since a double of an even-money shot and a 22-1 shot should come back at a little over $100, you are looking at a three-digit payoff here too. If so, you will be disappointed when the exacta comes back closer to $59.

When we said in Chapter 2 that a double combining horses with odds of 1-1 and 22-1 should pay $102.60, we did this by calculating the percentage of the double tickets sold on that combination suggested by the win-pool odds. In this case, 42.5 percent of all the double tickets sold used the 1 in the first race at 1-1, and 3.67 percent of those tickets used the 5 in the second at 22-1. That multiplies to 1.55 (42.5 x 3.67) percent of the double pool, for an after-takeout payoff of $102.60.

In an exacta, though, once number 1 has won the race at even money, number 5 is no longer 22-1 to finish second. He is still the longest shot among the four remaining candidates to finish second, but instead of being 22-1 in a pool where an even-money shot had accounted for 42.5 percent of the pool, he is now a bigger fish in a smaller pond, more like 14-1 than 22-1. It may be helpful to think of it as if there are two separate races: a five-horse race to see who will finish first, followed by a four-horse race to see who will run second. Since the favorite has been removed from the possibilities for that second race, everyone else's odds go down.

This can be even more pronounced in trifectas, where this same thing happens an additional time. With an eight-horse field, you have an eight-horse race for first, a seven-horse race for second, and a six-horse race for third, with everyone's win odds dropping through the subtraction of an already-placed starter. Returning to our sample race, suppose that the even-money favorite wins, the 2-1 second choice is second, and the 22-1 bomb is third. Your first reaction might be to call your travel agent, since you got that 22-1 shot to run third. You might think that you turned $2 into $4 with the winner, $4 into $12 with the 2-1 runner-up, and $12 into $276 with the 22-1 shot. In fact, you're not going to get much better than 22-1 for the whole trifecta.

Here's what happened. Once the even-money favorite won the race, the 2-1 shot effectively became a 7-10 shot to run second. (Instead of having 28 percent of the pool on him, with the subtraction of number 1's 42.5 percent of the win pool, he had 28/58 of the remaining pool, or nearly half.) And once he did that, the 22-1 shot was in only a three-horse race with the 4-1 shot and the 9-1 shot to finish third. Instead of being 4-1, 9-1, and 22-1, those three were closer to 2-5, 2-1, and 6-1 in the three-horse race for third place.

So your trifecta is going to come back around $59. Getting that 22-1 shot to run third was not quite the heroic feat it first seemed.

Another seeming anomaly illustrated above is how close together each pair of exacta payoffs involving two horses with disparate odds is, despite which one finishes first. It may seem counterintuitive that if a 2-1 beats a 4-1, the payoff is $23.80, but only $27.40 if the 4-1 beats the 2-1. Shouldn't it be something like twice as much? And shouldn't there be a vaster gap than the one between $59 and $98.50, depending on whether the 1-1 favorite wins or loses a photo finish with the 22-1 shot?

It feels like there should be, but the math says otherwise. Let's look at the latter example, remembering that the runner-up's effective win odds decrease with the subtraction of the winner. When the 1-1 shot beats the 22-1 shot, for exacta purposes it's as if a 1-1 shot beat only a 13-1, because the 22-1 shot's odds effectively plummet with the subtraction of the favorite from the four-horse race for second. When the 22-1 shot beats the 1-1 shot, though, the 1-1 shot becomes a 9-10 shot, only a slight reduction.

Note that in both cases you are still getting an inherent bonus over those adjusted win odds because you've theoretically cut the takeout from 15 to 10 percent by making two bets for the price of one with a 20 percent takeout in the exacta. Even so, it can take years to get used to the idea that it's not even twice as good for you in the exacta when the 22-1 shot noses out the 1-1 favorite.

Now let's create a similar chart for the trifecta, where there are 60 possible payoffs in a five-horse field:

TRIFECTA POOL

(Takeout: 15% WPS, 25% Trifecta; Breakage: NY rules)
Win odds: #1: 1-1; #2: 2-1; #3: 4-1; #4: 9-1; #5: 22-1

Trifecta	1st/2nd/3rd Win Odds	%Pool	$2 Tri Pays
1-2-3	1-1/2-1/4-1	12.21%	$ 12.20
1-2-4	1-1/2-1/9-1	6.10%	$ 24.40
1-2-5	1-1/2-1/22-1	2.63%	$ 56.50
1-3-2	1-1/4-1/2-1	8.79%	$ 17.00
1-3-4	1-1/4-1/9-1	2.64%	$ 56.50
1-3-5	1-1/4-1/22-1	1.14%	$ 131.50
1-4-2	1-1/9-1/2-1	3.63%	$ 41.20
1-4-3	1-1/9-1/4-1	2.18%	$ 68.50
1-4-5	1-1/9-1/22-1	0.47%	$ 319.00
1-5-2	1-1/22-1/2-1	1.43%	$ 105.00
1-5-3	1-1/22-1/4-1	0.86%	$ 175.00
1-5-4	1-1/22-1/9-1	0.43%	$ 350.53
Subtotal		42.50%	
2-1-3	2-1/1-1/4-1	9.79%	$ 15.20
2-1-4	2-1/1-1/9-1	4.90%	$ 30.60
2-1-5	2-1/1-1/22-1	2.11%	$ 71.00
2-3-1	2-1/4-1/1-1	5.22%	$ 28.60
2-3-4	2-1/4-1/9-1	1.05%	$ 143.50
2-3-5	2-1/4-1/22-1	0.45%	$ 332.50
2-4-1	2-1/9-1/1-1	2.26%	$ 66.20

Trifecta	1st/2nd/3rd Win Odds	%Pool	$2 Tri Pays
2-4-3	2-1/9-1/4-1	0.90%	$ 165.50
2-4-5	2-1/9-1/22-1	0.20%	$ 768.00
2-5-1	2-1/22-1/1-1	0.91%	$ 165.50
2-5-3	2-1/22-1/4-1	0.36%	$ 413.50
2-5-4	2-1/22-1/9-1	0.18%	$ 827.00
Subtotal		28.33%	
3-1-2	4-1/1-1/2-1	6.09%	$ 24.60
3-1-4	4-1/1-1/9-1	1.83%	$ 82.00
3-1-5	4-1/1-1/22-1	0.79%	$ 190.00
3-2-1	4-1/2-1/1-1	4.51%	$ 33.20
3-2-4	4-1/2-1/9-1	0.90%	$ 166.20
3-2-5	4-1/2-1/22-1	0.39%	$ 385.00
3-4-1	4-1/9-1/1-1	0.99%	$ 151.00
3-4-2	4-1/9-1/2-1	0.66%	$ 226.50
3-4-5	4-1/9-1/22-1	0.09%	$1,750.60
3-5-1	4-1/22-1/1-1	0.40%	$ 372.50
3-5-2	4-1/22-1/2-1	0.27%	$ 559.00
3-5-4	4-1/22-1/9-1	0.08%	$1,864.00
Subtotal		17.00%	
4-1-2	9-1/1-1/2-1	2.28%	$ 65.50
4-1-3	9-1/1-1/4-1	1.37%	$ 109.50
4-1-5	9-1/1-1/22-1	0.30%	$ 507.00
4-2-1	9-1/2-1/1-1	1.77%	$ 84.50
4-2-3	9-1/2-1/4-1	0.71%	$ 211.50
4-2-5	9-1/2-1/22-1	0.15%	$ 981.00
4-3-1	9-1/4-1/1-1	0.90%	$ 166.50
4-3-2	9-1/4-1/2-1	0.60%	$ 249.50

Trifecta	1st/2nd/3rd Win Odds	%Pool	$2 Tri Pays
4-3-5	9-1/4-1/22-1	0.08%	$1,929.00
4-5-1	9-1/22-1/1-1	0.17%	$ 910.00
4-5-2	9-1/22-1/2-1	0.11%	$1,365.00
4-5-3	9-1/22-1/4-1	0.07%	$2,275.00
Subtotal		8.50%	
5-1-2	22-1/1-1/2-1	0.85%	$ 176.00
5-1-3	22-1/1-1/4-1	0.51%	$ 293.50
5-1-4	22-1/1-1/9-1	0.26%	$ 587.00
5-2-1	22-1/2-1/1-1	0.67%	$ 222.50
5-2-3	22-1/2-1/4-1	0.27%	$ 556.00
5-2-4	22-1/2-1/9-1	0.14%	$1,112.00
5-3-1	22-1/4-1/1-1	0.35%	$ 432.50
5-3-2	22-1/4-1/2-1	0.23%	$ 649.00
5-3-4	22-1/4-1/9-1	0.07%	$2,163.00
5-4-1	22-1/9-1/1-1	0.16%	$ 958.00
5-4-2	22-1/9-1/2-1	0.10%	$1,437.00
5-4-3	22-1/9-1/4-1	0.06%	$2,395.00
Subtotal		3.67%	
GRAND TOTAL		100.00%	

Having 60 rather than 20 possible outcomes opens up the range of payoffs. Whereas our exactas ranged from a low of $7.60 for the 1-2 to $494.50 for the 5-4, here the spread is from $12.20 for the 1-2-3 to $2,395 for the 5-4-3.

Ranking the 60 payoffs from lowest to highest reveals some interesting things, including a crucial strategic point in intrarace exotics:

- The seven shortest-priced trifectas (1-2-3, 2-1-3, 1-3-2, 1-2-4, 3-1-2, 2-3-1, 2-1-4) account for a whopping 53 percent of the pool.
- The 20 shortest-priced trifectas all include the favorite.
- The 36 combinations including the favorite account for 92 percent of the pool, while the 24 combinations excluding the favorite account for just 8 percent of the money bet in the pool, including the 10 highest payoffs.

In a win pool, an even-money favorite appears on 42.5 percent of the tickets, but this rises to 92 percent in the trifecta pool, because the favorite can appear in the second or third slots as well as on top. This increasingly high percentage of tickets including the favorite in each pool, however, ultimately creates an imbalance and an opportunity. While even-money favorites win at a rate (42 to 46 percent of the time) comparable to the percentage of the pool they attract, they finish first, second, or third closer to 75 than 92 percent of the time. In other words, favorites are overbet "underneath" in trifectas, so trifecta players are frequently going to receive overlaid payoffs when they can get the favorite to finish worse than third.

This situation may be even better than it looks above, because bettors may well overbet favorites even more than the mathematical model suggests they should. (This is a purely anecdotal observation that cannot be tested, as no one retains the millions of possible trifecta payoffs it would be necessary to analyze.) It seems logical, however, that the combination of limited bankrolls and lazy betting strategies such as boxes would lead to a further overuse of favorites.

An undercapitalized trifecta player who makes four-horse boxes for $24 a race probably designates the favorite as one of his four horses almost every single time. Such players do not have the bankroll to play against the favorite time after time and to collect nothing more often than not. They include the favorite even when they don't particularly like him because they live in fear that the favorite will run third behind two of their clever selections.

Deciding what to do with a favorite is always a crucial piece of any handicapping or betting strategy, perhaps more so in intrarace wagers than anywhere else. While a pick four or pick six can still have a five-digit payoff with one or two favorites in the sequence, a favorite's presence will severely depress the exotic payoffs on a single race.

The point is not that you should recklessly or routinely pitch favorites from intrarace exotics, but that the time to step in may well be when you think the favorite is likelier to run poorly than his odds might suggest. Again, this is a matter of having an opinion and using the exotics to amplify its value.

Intrarace Handicapping

As noted in the very first sentence of this book, the aim of this volume is not to promote any particular method of selecting horses, but instead to explore how exotic wagering can maximize the value of your opinions regardless of how you arrived at them. In intrarace wagers, however, there is a unique handicapping component that is absent from both straight and multirace betting: You need to come up with the second, third, and even fourth finishers in a race.

Some handicappers will not see this as a big difference from whatever method they use to select winners. They would argue that coming up with the second-place finisher is simply a matter of finding the winner of a race that no longer includes the first-place finisher. These handicappers would contend that if they think three horses are the best win propositions, these same horses should be combined in exactas or trifectas because they are by definition still the best prospects for both the primary race and the subraces for second or third.

My own approach to handicapping, especially for intrarace purposes, is somewhat different—not necessarily better or worse, but perhaps worth considering if you routinely combine only your top win candidates in intrarace wagers. I believe strongly in speed figures as the best measure of a horse's ability under optimal circumstances. However, I do not believe that races are decided as if they are run with 10-foot walls separating the horses and that all you must do is decide who will "throw" or "deliver" the best number today.

I believe instead that horse races are organic events in which any horse's performance can be helped or hindered by the way the race is run, especially in terms of the pace of the race. This becomes particularly relevant when structuring an intrarace play, because while a superior horse may well overcome pace issues to prevail, the remaining order of finish may be more directly affected by pace. Horses you might include or exclude when considering who will win are not automatically the right inclusions or throwouts for "underneath" purposes.

Take the obvious case of a race in which the two logical favorites tower over the field in terms of their best performances, but both are intractable front-runners and there are other need-the-lead types in the race. Let's say you're convinced that the closers in the field are so slow that even if the two favorites hook up early, no one's going to catch them both and one of them will last for the victory. But isn't it likely that the loser of the early duel will be so enervated that he may well tire badly in the lane and one of those hapless 12-1 closers will clunk up for second? It may seem counterintuitive, but in such a situation, the second favorite may have a greater chance of winning the race—if he pops the gate and gets loose on his own—than he does of finishing second under any scenario.

Conversely, a field containing very little early speed might feature a favored stretch-runner who routinely trails early and comes flying late. If you can envision a setup where one or two of his opponents may be able to get away with very easy fractions, the favorite may be a good bet-against in the win position but should probably still be included underneath.

In either situation, you are giving yourself an advantage by awarding greater or lesser emphasis to a horse in the win position as opposed to the other slots, because the public is probably giving him equal favor in all positions. This is yet another reason always to question whether simply boxing your selections is the most efficient way to structure your intrarace exotic plays.

Exacta Strategies

Let's look at some of the reasons you might play exactas in a race, evaluate their soundness, and then see how the good ideas can be translated into mechanically optimal wagers that will maximize their potential. If you asked bettors who just finished playing some exactas why they chose this race and pool, most of the answers would probably fall into one of these four categories:

1. I really couldn't separate the top three or four horses in here, so I boxed them.
2. I kind of like a longshot in here and I'm trying to catch a big number.

3. I think there's a way to improve the win odds of the horse I like.

4. I think the favorite or favorites are vulnerable, or I think the race will unfold in a way where running style could be more important than sheer ability.

Let's first review why we hope that others come up with Answers 1 or 2. Boxing several favorites in a race is a concession that you have no opinion of any value and is a formula for slow, steady losses. You will frequently lose money even when you cash, and by betting every combination in equal value, you will simply end up rooting for the highest-priced and least-likely outcome.

As for Answer 2, keying a longshot with either "all" or the favorites is another long-term money-loser. Wheeling horses is nothing more than playing roulette, and dilutes their value.

Answer 3 is finally a good reason. The central premise of parimutuel wagering is to get a better price from the other bettors than something deserves to be. The two ways to do that are to wait around for a bargain in the win pool and be content with infrequent action and slight advantages, or to try to create such situations for yourself through the exotics. It's nice if we can find a legitimate 2-1 shot going off at 3-1, but nicer still if we can turn him into 7-1 through the exotics without doubling the risk.

Consider our now familiar friend Our Hero at 4-1. We have already seen that wheeling him in the exacta is a terrible idea and that taking him on top of only the even-money and 2-1 favorites provides merely a small enhancement to the win price. But what if we have a more valuable second opinion about the race? There are at least three such scenarios under which we might try to improve on that 4-1.

The first is if we don't think the even-money favorite is any kind of cinch to beat the others for second and is worth playing against at a short price. We might now either split our investment between a win bet and the following exacta play, or live a bit more dangerously and skip the win bet altogether. We might take the same $20 we were going to bet to win and instead invest it this way:

$14 on the 3-2 exacta paying $27.40   Return = $191.80
$ 4 on the 3-4 exacta paying $91.50   Return = $183.00
$ 2 on the 3-5 exacta paying $213.00   Return = $213.00

Instead of getting back $100 on a $20 win bet, we are now getting back between $183 and $213 regardless of who runs second, so long as it isn't the favorite. We have approximately doubled our return, getting 8-1 or 9-1 instead of 4-1, and do not believe we have doubled our risk.

It is even more common for you to end up disliking the second choice, rather than the favorite, and while it's somewhat less valuable to discard a 2-1 than a 1-1 shot, you may have a higher confidence factor and strike rate. Let's invest that $20 again, this time leaving out the 2 instead of the 1:

$16 on the 3-1 exacta paying $18.20   Return = $145.60
$ 3 on the 3-4 exacta paying $91.50   Return = $137.25
$ 1 on the 3-5 exacta paying $213.00   Return = $106.50

If you're betting more than $20, you can more effectively smooth out those potential returns to bring them closer together. They're not as flashy as those where we played against the favorite, but still represent a significant improvement over the $100 win-bet return.

This latter play may seem cockeyed because you are betting 80 percent on the combination with the favorite in order to equalize the potential returns. What if you legitimately think the two longshots have better chances of finishing second than their odds suggest?

This is where strategic decisions get tricky. There are at least two ways to go. First, you might decide that you're willing to get only a $100 return, the same as the win price on Our Hero, if the favorite runs second, and you would bet less on that combination to give yourself a little more on the others. You might opt for something like this:

$11 on the 3-1 exacta paying $18.20   Return = $100.10
$ 6 on the 3-4 exacta paying $91.50   Return = $274.50
$ 3 on the 3-5 exacta paying $213.00   Return = $319.50

Now you've made a tradeoff. You're taking the win-pool price of 4-1 if the favorite runs second, getting no improvement in price while assuming the risk of ruin if the despised 2-1 second choice runs second. But you've picked up the opportunity to get a return of between 12-1 and 15-1 if you can get one of the two longshots to run second.

Whether or not that's a good tradeoff boils down to how much you like those two longshots.

Whatever decision you make, you're thinking harder and better than the vast majority of your competition in the exacta pool. Even many of those who share your opinion that Our Hero is the right key horse are hurting themselves and helping your prices by either boxing him with both favorites or wheeling him and trying to get lucky. You're already ahead of the game.

Now let's consider Answer 4 from above, from the person whose entire reason for playing a race is a dislike of the favorites or an emphasis on pace and running style rather than simple ability. Our example race is not a particularly likely spot for such a play, because you will rarely find yourself taking a position that the horses who have attracted a combined 70 percent of the win pool will both run worse than second. Also, in our five-horse field, pitching both favorites would leave you with only three horses and six exacta combinations. Still, if you really did have good reason to play against them both, it could be rewarding. Rather than boxing the 3-4-5 and rooting for a 5-4, we might weight the six combinations as follows with a $32 investment:

$10 on the 3-4 exacta paying $ 91.50   Return = $457.50
$ 5 on the 3-5 exacta paying $ 213.00   Return = $532.50
$ 9 on the 4-3 exacta paying $ 101.00   Return = $454.50
$ 2 on the 4-5 exacta paying $ 469.00   Return = $469.00
$ 4 on the 5-3 exacta paying $ 247.00   Return = $494.00
$ 2 on the 5-4 exacta paying $ 494.50   Return = $494.50

Again, investing more than $32 would allow you to equalize the returns better, but in this example you're investing $32 to get back between $454.50 and $532.50, a return of between 13-1 and 16-1. If you believe there is a better than 1 in 12 chance that both favorites could be out of the exacta, you've made a good bet on a proposition not available through conventional betting or the WPS pools.

In general, exacta pools do not reflect as many of the bankroll-related betting inefficiencies offered in more complex pools, for a variety of reasons: the smaller number of available combinations; the relatively affordable cost of buying them; the fact that exacta probables are posted during betting while trifecta and superfecta probables are not; and the sheer size of the pools, which are usually larger than the win pool. It could even be argued that due to their greater size, exacta pools may offer a truer estimation of how much the public "likes" each horse than the win pool.

In any case, it is rare for an exacta payoff to be wildly out of line with the win odds on the first two finishers, especially at larger tracks. There are, however, some minor and consistent exacta-betting inefficiencies worth keeping in mind:

- Combinations likeliest to have been hit using three- and four-horse boxes or wheels tend to be underlaid relative to the win odds. The combination of the second and third choices in a race often seems to pay a little less than it should, probably because of the prevalence of three-horse boxes, especially in a race where there is a favorite at 3-2 or less. If the second and third choices are 4-1 and 6-1, the exacta may pay less than those prices would suggest simply because so many people are locked into boxing the top three choices. (This a theme to which we will return in multirace betting, where a horse's ordinal rank in the betting is often more important than his win price.)
- Combinations that use a heavy favorite on top with a big longshot in second are often similarly short, in this case due to wheeling. So many unsophisticated bettors think the presence of a strong favorite is an invitation to wheel and root for chaos that combinations like 4-5 over 30-1 rarely pay what they should.

- All that boxing and wheeling that creates the two underlay situations just mentioned has to have a flip side. The corresponding sweet spot may be in combinations involving the third, fourth, and fifth choices in a field of eight or fewer, and the third through seventh choices in larger fields. These are combinations left out of all those $12 and $24 boxes that include the two favorites, and the value of these midpriced horses is not negatively impacted by wheels.

- This may seem contradictory to some of the above, but there is a frequent phenomenon where an exacta with a heavy favorite finishing second pays more generously than you would think, especially if the winner is not the second or third choice. A $30 winner over a 3-5 shot "should" pay only $50 (5.67 percent of the pool over 53 percent of the remaining pool = 3.19 percent of the total pool = $50.14), but will often come back paying $60 or more. The reason for this somewhat illogical occurrence is that this combination is out of the purview of most boxes and wheels, and that people using 14-1 shots on top may tend to be a little greedy and shoot for bigger exacta payoffs by talking themselves out of using a legitimate favorite underneath.

It might seem unadventurous to hook up a clever, subtle 14-1 shot with a short-priced horse for second, but if you believe the favorite is better than 50-50 to run second if your horse wins, you should be allocating some of your investment to that $60-or-better exacta instead of just a win bet at 14-1. If the favorite was 3-5 to win the race, isn't it perhaps worth taking 6-5 on him to beat the rest of the field, which no longer includes your brilliant 14-1 shot?

Stupid Exacta Tricks

The examples above using bets totaling $20 or $32 imply that these are bare minimums necessary to buy the various combinations, and at adequately weighted levels, to ensure similar returns. For the person who bets more like $100 or $500 a race, it's easy enough to multiply them by 5 or 10. However, players with medium-to-large bankrolls may also want to consider these small plays as total investments for a category of wagers many serious handicapping authors frown upon entirely: fun bets, also known as action bets.

In theory, the only time you should bet is when you're getting the best of it, receiving favorable odds for carefully considered opinions, even if that means sitting on your hands for a race or the majority of a card. In reality, though, it is unreasonable to ask anyone but the most disciplined full-time bettor, protecting his bankroll as if he might miss a meal if he makes a loose bet, to behave this way. Someone who works full time and gets to the track or simulcast parlor once a week can't really be expected to make only one bet all day.

Besides, there is something to be said for having even a token bet going on a race just to force yourself to watch it with enough interest to perhaps notice something that will be important in the future. There is also a case to be made that if you have a tiny notion about a horse or a race, one not fully developed or considered enough to merit your normal full-sized bet, you should get a little something back if you're right, if only to keep from spending the rest of the day beating yourself up over passing it. Even if such bets prove no better than a break-even proposition in the long run, their mental-health value may be a sufficiently mitigating factor.

Exactas work well for these action bets because they are

relatively cheap. If you start fooling around with a trifecta or super in a semi-whimsical action situation, you may find yourself quickly spending as much as you would on a real bet. For $20 or $30, though, you might have some fun with what I think of as "stupid exacta tricks."

One is to take a race where you're mildly skeptical of the favorites, but otherwise too confused to construct an aggressive play, and key two wing-and-a-prayer longshots with four or five others in the field, dumping the favorites. Let's say the odds for a 10-horse field look something like this:

1: 4-1   2: 17-1   3: 6-1   4: 21-1   5: 16-1
6: 12-1   7: 5-2   8: 19-1   9: 75-1   10: 3-1

Let's say our half-baked ideas are that number 4 at 21-1 and number 5 at 16-1 are not out of the question. We might begin by dumping the three favorites, the 1, 7, and 10, then also eliminate the completely hopeless 9 at 75-1. You could construct a tiny play consisting of two exacta part-wheels:

$1 exacta 4,5/2,3,4,5,6,8 = $10
$1 exacta 2,3,4,5,6,8/4,5 = $10

For $20, we get a dollar of the exacta if either the 4 or 5 runs either first or second and the three chalks and the 75-1 shot are all out of the first two positions. We even get the 4-5 and 5-4 combinations an extra time each because these appear on both tickets, just in case both of our horses come through. We have 18 of the possible 90 exacta combinations in the race, and our return for $20 is going to range from about $115 for a 3-5 to $450 for a 4-8. If by some miracle it's a 4-5 or a 5-4, we're looking at about $900.

If that happens, you'll kick yourself a little for not elevating your investment to a full-sized bet, but not as hard as you would be kicking if you had passed the race altogether. Granted, if the favorite runs second to your 21-1 shot, you'll get nothing. If this is going to ruin your day, up your investment to $24 and take $2 to win on each half-baked key. The idea, though, is a little entertainment and a little insanity insurance, not to cover every eventuality on a race you deemed unworthy of a real bet.

A section of this book with the word *stupid* in its title seems the appropriate place to begin and end any discussion of the exacta's dimwitted cousin, the quinella. The exacta got its name because you must buy a combination containing the "exact" 1-2 order of finish. In the quinella, however, you win whether the order of finish is 1-2 or 2-1.

The only appeal the quinella ever had was that it offered bettors with the smallest bankrolls a chance to play the equivalent of exacta boxes and part-wheels at half the price. A $1, three-horse exacta box of numbers 1, 3, and 5 costs $6 because there are six combinations (1-3, 1-5, 3-1, 3-5, 5-1, 5-3). A three-horse, $1 quinella box costs only $3 because there are only three possible combinations—1-3, 1-5, and 3-5—since a 1-3 is the same as a 3-1, a 1-5 is a 5-1, and a 3-5 covers a 5-3.

With the gradual lowering of exacta minimums from $2 to $1, the quinella has little reason for continued existence, as there are not many 21st-century horseplayers who can afford to spend $3 but not $6. The quinella, however, is worse than merely duplicative. By covering both a 1-3 and a 3-1 outcome on a single 1-3 ticket, the quinella forces you to accept a single payoff unaffected by which horse wins. This robs you of the flexibility to emphasize your opinion one way or the other. If you think Horse A is a cinch and Horse B is an interesting possibility for second, an A-B quinella wastes half your investment by equally rewarding those who liked B to beat A. The payoff is always going to be smaller than the exacta because there are only half as many possible outcomes, and what would have been separate payoffs on A-B and B-A have been combined.

Unless you're down to your last $3, avoid the bet.

Trifecta Strategies

Now the truly exotic wagering begins.

The trifecta in one sense is nothing more than an exacta with a third leg, and some people think of it that way—a win bet combined with an exacta on the 2-3 finishers or an exacta parlayed to a win bet on who will finish third. That may be conceptually helpful in thinking about payoffs and possibilities, but the bet is best approached as an entirely separate creature.

Inefficiency in the pool becomes much more of an issue with trifectas than exactas. Whereas exacta prices closely match win odds because of large pools and limited combinations, trifectas have both smaller pools and more combinations over which the money is spread. There are going to be a greater number of inefficiently overbet combinations as well as more neglected ones. The tradeoff is that trifecta prices are not posted during the betting, making the payoff a surprise revealed only when the results are official.

The trifecta was the first common multiple wager involving three or more horses in American racing, and almost every current horseplayer made his first score on the bet because it was once the only wager on the menu with a realistic possibility of a four-digit payoff. In New York, for example, throughout the 1970's and early 1980's there was only one trifecta a day, on the last race, and it became the focus of the afternoon for many players who wanted to bet a little to make a lot.

Today nearly every race at every track has both exacta and trifecta betting, creating a crucial choice for intrarace exotics players: Which do I want to play on this race—the exacta, the trifecta, or both? Many players make the choice based on only three factors—bankroll, habit, and greed, all of them poor criteria.

Bankroll is an issue because the inclusion of a third-place finisher causes a steep increase in the price of a similar play. A five-horse exacta box triples in price if played as a five-horse trifecta box. Keying one horse back and forth with four others is eight exacta bets, but keying one horse in all positions of a trifecta with four others is 36 bets. These become crucial differences for the "average" bettor whose total handle is between $20 and $40 a race.

Habit would seem like an unlikely motive, but it is surprising how many bettors unfettered by minimum-bankroll issues say they play one bet significantly more than the other. Neither bet is intrinsically superior to the other, and preference may well stem from early experience. People who began betting with scarce funds and found trifectas difficult to corral may have forsaken them and failed to reconsider them as their handicapping and bankrolls improved. Others who may have made a defining early score on a trifecta may still be chasing them even though they play them poorly.

The correct answer is that sometimes one bet makes sense for you more than the other in a particular handicapping situation.

With the trifecta, the crucial new factor is the inclusion of the third-place finisher, and that becomes the crux of the decision about which pool to play. Some of the questions you might ask yourself when choosing between the bets include the following:

1. Do I really have a handle on this race or am I stabbing with a couple of notions?
2. Do I have a good idea about how the race will be run, or just a sense of who the most talented horses are?
3. Can I confidently eliminate half the field from running third or am I really just hitting the "all" button for third and trying to get lucky?

Let's consider each of these questions a bit more closely.

The question of whether you have a small notion or a truly good idea about a race is one that colors every decision a handicapper makes—race selection, size of investment, pool selection, real bet versus fun bet. It's something learned only through experience as you develop an inner ear to be honest about the strength and quality of your opinion in any given race.

There's a subtle but crucial difference between being completely at sea over a race and having it under control without having a specific selection. If you're just lost, a trifecta is probably a terrible idea. You might want to make an action bet with your small notions, play two or three of them in a simpler bet like a daily double or exacta, or pass entirely, instead of trying to be precise down to third place. This is different from a race where you actually have a handle on the contenders but just don't see any thrilling opportunities. In that case you might end up focusing on the one horse whose price seems unusually generous and perhaps constructing a trifecta play around him because you have good convictions about which other horses can or can't be part of the number.

One useful self-test is asking yourself to imagine how the race might be run. Forcing yourself at least to consider this may reveal whether you have identified the contenders and considered what factors about today's race might work to the advantage of some and not others. If instead you find yourself with nothing but a lot of question marks and horses you can't either endorse or reject, betting on the 1-2-3 order of finish is probably just too ambitious.

Eliminating horses from contention becomes as valuable a skill as any other when you're playing trifectas. It avoids putting yourself in the position of effectively playing an exacta and then hitting the "all" button for third, and allows you to move remaining contenders higher up on your ticket. As discussed earlier, getting a longshot up for third is never as valuable as it might seem.

Eliminating horses from your trifecta ticket entirely also opens the door to your doing the one thing most trifecta players fail to do: having the trifecta for more than the standard $1. Perhaps in a holdover from the era when the trifecta was the lone exotic opportunity of the day, many players want to "have" the trifecta, and pronounce themselves smart for doing so rather than considering whether casting a wide net to come up with a single $1 combo was really the best way to go.

The majority of trifecta investments probably fall into one of the following five categories: small boxes, small part-wheels, big boxes, big part-wheels, and aggressive punches. Let's look at the mechanics and the pros and cons of each.

1. *Small Boxes.* A surprising number of bettors will play a single trifecta box if they "like" three horses in a race, and then moan about having suffered a terrible injustice when they run 1-2 or 1-3 but not 1-2-3. Filling out two-thirds of the combination makes them feel close to success and tantalizes them to repeat this behavior.

   The problem is that they may not appreciate the degree of difficulty in what they are attempting. In a typical eight-horse field, there are 336 (8 x 7 x 6) possible trifecta outcomes. Buying a single three-horse box gives you only six of those 336 combos, or one of the possible 56 boxes. In addition to skimpy coverage, you are requiring that all three of your horses fire their best shot, and that is a great deal to ask. It's far more common for two of them to run their usual races while the third either throws in a clunker or is compromised in some fashion.

   You really haven't come particularly close if two of your three horses are part of the trifecta. In that eight-horse field with 336 possible outcomes, there are 96 separate outcomes that include any two of your three horses, but only the six in your single box with all three.

   Stepping up to a four-horse box quadruples your costs and coverage. You're now buying the equivalent of four of those 56 possible boxes; if your horses are the 1, 3, 5, and 7, you are effectively buying a 1-3-5, a 1-3-7, a 1-5-7, and a 3-5-7 box all on one ticket. There might be situations where you truly believe that only four horses can possibly fill out the top three slots and that the other four horses in the race are hopeless to hit the board. Still, it's worth questioning whether this is the best use of 24 separate bets. You're being wasteful by not emphasizing any single horse or combination over any other, giving each horse an equal chance to win or finish in the money. Also, remember that 18 of your 24 combinations involve a single horse who must finish 1-2-3, and your only additional coverage is a single three-horse box.

One alternative for the modestly bankrolled player who wants about $24 worth of trifecta-box action is to consider requiring two of your horses to hit the board, which allows you to be looser about including some others. For the same $24 it costs for a 1-2-3-4 box, you could make the following four boxes: 1-2-3, 1-2-4, 1-2-5, and 1-2-6. The tradeoff is that while both the 1 and the 2 must now be in the money, you have picked up two more horses who can be the other part of the trifecta, and in any position. This can be an effective little play if you think there's a solid favorite who is likely to be in the money and your other key horse is an interesting longshot. It also qualifies as a stupid trifecta trick if you want to take a $24 flyer on a couple of high-priced but wacky notions.

2. *Small Part-Wheels.* Sticking with the previous example for a moment: What if, instead of making a simple four-horse box where 75 percent of your combinations require one horse to hit the board, you decided to focus on that horse even more? By changing the parameters of your bet to require that this key horse must finish first or second, for the same $24 you could buy yourself some extra coverage in the third position. Instead of a 1-3-5-7 box, you might now buy the following two $1 part-wheels, each of which costs $12:

1/3,5,7/3,4,5,6,7
3,5,7/1/3,4,5,6,7

(The "/" sign in part-wheel notation is a separator between positions. In calling out a part-wheel, the slash should be articulated as the word *with*—for example, "One-dollar trifecta part-wheel, one *with* three, five, seven *with* three, four, five, six, seven.")

A four-horse box and this pair of part-wheels have 12 of their 24 combinations in common. The difference is that in the four-horse box, your other 12 combinations are the six involving number 1 finishing third and the six excluding the 1 entirely while adding the 3-5-7 box. In the part-wheel, you have replaced these 12 combinations with 12 new ones involving the 4 or 6 finishing third.

You have 24 combinations either way, but you may be in a stronger position with the part-wheels. You have taken a bit more of a stand with your key horse, requiring that he run first or second, sacrificing only those combinations where he finishes precisely third or the small comfort of the single 3-5-7 box if he's out of the money. What you get in exchange is the addition of two more horses who can finish third, presumably at bigger prices than your key horse or next three choices.

This assumes that there is a clear hierarchical ranking in your mind under which the 1 is very likely to finish first or second and the 3, 5, and 7 are clearly superior to the 4 and 6. The key is to match your true opinion to your executed bet. A slight difference in your hierarchy would suggest a different play. What if, for example, your hierarchy had only two levels: that number 1 and number 3 should both run well and one of them should win, and that you can't really pick apart the 4, 5, 6, and 7. Now you might want to consider a different pair of part-wheels:

$$1,3/1,3/4,5,6,7 = 8 \text{ bets}$$
$$1,3/4,5,6,7/1,3 = 8 \text{ bets}$$

You have reduced your cost by a third, with 16 rather than 24 combinations. You now require that both the 1 and the 3 win or hit the board, but you've picked up tickets where the 4 or the 6 can run second as well as third. You could either put that extra $8 back in your pocket, or you could buy the first part-wheel for $2 rather than $1. If you're going to be right, with your two key horses running 1-2, why not get rewarded and paid double?

3. *Big Boxes.* Boxing five horses in a trifecta requires 60 base bets ($60 at a $1 minimum), while six will run you $120 and seven horses cost $210. By now, we should know by heart the litany of inherent drawbacks to boxing—you are giving all your horses equal weight, you are not discriminating between horses who can actually win the race and those whose best hope is to clunk up for third, and your big box contains plenty of money-losing "winning" combinations if it includes the two favorites.

   Keeping all that in mind, the big box might be an attractive strategy in one situation: where your strongest opinion about a race is the vulnerability of the favorites, and you honestly cannot draw fine lines among the remaining legitimate contenders. Given the inherent value in eliminating favorites from trifecta combinations, you might not want to zigzag your way out of a fat trifecta by relegating some of the longshots to second-only or third-only status.

Let's say there's a 10-horse field where you have very good reason to believe the two favorites might both finish off the board. Maybe the two chalks, the 1 and 2, are both committed front-runners who might duel each other into defeat, especially since the 9 and 10 are also front-runners who will be gunned to the fore from their outside posts.

How do you want to invest your $120 on your opinion that there's going to be a cavalry charge to the wire involving the six horses in the middle of the gate? You could make a 3-4-5-6-7-8 trifecta box, but perhaps you're worried about one of the favorites hanging on for third. For the same investment, you could make a 4 x 6 x 8-horse part-wheel, using only four of those six horses in the win position, all of them for second, and adding the two favorites for third. Such a ticket would read: 3,4,5,6/3,4,5,6,7,8/1,2,3,4,5,6,7,8. (Remember that this ticket uses 4 x 6 x 8 horses but costs only 4 x 5 x 6 combinations because we subtract one horse from the second position and two from the third position to avoid repeating digits.)

It boils down to a choice: Are you more concerned about the 7 or 8 finishing first or the 1 or 2 finishing third? It's a question of value as well as likelihood: A third-place finish by one of the favorites will depress the trifecta price, so you may want to lean toward fuller coverage with their both being off the board, since that was your initial interest in the entire proposition.

4. *Big Part-Wheels and Key Part-Wheels.* In the example above, a 4 x 6 x 8 part-wheel might be justified because 96 of your 120 combinations involve both favorites finishing out of the trifecta, and every one of those is going to pay the necessary $240 for $2 for you to break even. Quite a few of them will produce payoffs in the four-digit range. In general, though, these extended part-wheels can be far less rewarding because of their high cost and the number of combinations you are buying, and you will be lucky to get your money back even if they come in.

Suppose that in this same hypothetical race you made a 4 x 6 x 8 part-wheel for $120 where you included the two favorites in your first tier of horses and your ticket looked like this:

1,2,3,4/1,2,3,4,5,6/1,2,3,4,5,6,7,8

You still have to get a $240-for-$2 payoff just to break even, and now half of your combinations involve one of the two favorites winning the race while only 30 of them have both favorites out of the money. You will cash this ticket often, but frequently for a loss.

An alternative to boxes and extended part-wheels is to key a horse in two or three positions, effectively surrounding him with your remaining contenders. For half the cost of that six-horse box, you might pick one of the six horses as your key, demand that he hit the board, and make three part-wheels as follows:

3/4,5,6,7,8/4,5,6,7,8
4,5,6,7,8/3/4,5,6,7,8
4,5,6,7,8/4,5,6,7,8/3

Each of these part-wheels contains 20 unit bets, for a total of 60 rather than the 120 required by a six-horse box.

You could similarly reduce the cost of that 4 x 6 x 8 part-wheel by keying on one of your four first-tier horses as follows:

3/4,5,6/1,2,4,5,6,7,8
4,5,6/3/1,2,4,5,6,7,8
4,5,6/1,2,4,5,6,7,8/3

Each of these requires 18 bets for a total of 54 rather than 120 combinations. (Note that the math on figuring the cost of these key part-wheels is a little different. A 1 x 3 x 7 part-wheel in this case reduces to only 1 x 3 x 6 combinations because the key horse [number 3] is not repeated in the other positions. So we subtract only from the third position, where the horses from the second position are repeated.)

The biggest problem with any of these plays is the volume of combinations you are buying relative to the possibility of a modest return. Even the $54 play above is a likely loser if your key horse and one or more of your second-tier choices include the favorites in the race. The wide-net approach only makes sense if you are trying to reel in large payoffs by playing against the public choices.

5. *Aggressive Punches.* The trifecta was the most exotic bet on most American racing menus for so long that many players, especially those who came of age as horseplayers in the 1970's and 1980's, still think of it as a bet where the whole idea is to "have" it, even if that means buying 60 or 120 combinations to get one winning $1 ticket. That may be the right approach if your bankroll is severely limited (in which case you probably should be playing exactas anyway), or when you are playing against the favorites. Many horseplayers, however, do not even consider the possibility of buying far fewer trifecta combinations in higher denominations. The same player who may feel comfortable making $10 or $20 exacta combinations may never bet more than a $1 trifecta. In doing so, such players are not only consistently nibbling away at their profits, but depriving themselves of the chance to make the significant scores that will sustain them through lean times and tip the ledger in their favor at year's end.

Even the $24-a-race player should consider some aggressive punches rather than the usual $1 four-horse box or $24 worth of part-wheels. Instead of a 1-2-3-4 box for $1, he might step out a little bit by focusing on how he really thinks the race might turn out and betting accordingly. If number 1 is the horse you like to win, and number 3 is the mildly interesting longshot you're betting on, you might consider an alternative like this:

$1 trifecta box	1-2-3	Cost: $6
$1 trifecta box	1-3-4	Cost $6
$3 trifecta part-wheel	1/3/2,4	Cost: $6
$3 trifecta part-wheel	1/2,4/3	Cost $6

This way, if things turn out ideally, you would have $4 ($1 from the box, $3 from the part-wheel) on your preferred combinations. The combinations you are sacrificing by not making the four-horse box are only the two boxes that don't contain both the 1 and the 3—the 1-2-4 box and the 2-3-4 box. You're not going to jump off a bridge if one of those comes in, but you've quadrupled your return when what you really like comes in.

Trifecta players are so fixated on "having it," and perhaps so wedded to early memories of having $1 worth of a $1,000 trifecta, that they seem to forget there is more than one way of cashing for $500 on a trifecta: In addition to having a buck of the $1,000 payout, you could have a $200 number five times or a $100 number 10 times. If you're thinking of keying one horse over three others in $20 exactas, why wouldn't you at least consider keying the same horse over those three in $10 trifectas for the same $60? There will be times when one of your horses runs second and a stranger beats you for third, but when you do hit, you'll be rewarded.

This kind of thinking may be increasingly useful as field size continues to wane in American racing. Six-horse races that may be completely unappetizing for win bets and unexciting for exactas may be opportunities for aggressive trifecta punches if you have a single good idea underneath.

A race at Aqueduct on February 26, 2006, provides a useful example. It was a maiden race for New York-breds with a pair of obvious, unassailable favorites: Ferocious Fires, a fast-working, well-bred first-time starter who took strong betting action to go off as the 2.10-1 favorite, and Midtown South, second in two straight starts at this level in fast races, earning him the top figures in the field. Without Ferocious Fires in the race he would have been an overwhelming favorite, but the high expectations surrounding the first-timer made him the 2.40-1 second choice.

The rest of the field was a sorry collection of slow-working firsters taking no money and career maidens who had failed multiple chances to run anywhere near as fast as Midtown South already had. A friend of mine, however, pointed out one interesting horse in this group: Funny Connection, a Florida shipper with an obscure trainer and jockey, who had been getting thrashed in open-company races at Gulfstream but whose figures in defeat were as good as anyone's beyond the two favorites. Funny Connection was 41-1.

My friend began moaning before the race about what a shame it was that his horse had drawn such a tough spot for his local debut, where realistically his best chance was to run third behind the two favorites, or maybe second if Ferocious Fires failed to fire ferociously. At 41-1 he had to bet anyway, so he invested a token $60, making a $20 win bet and boxing Funny Connection with the two favorites in $10 exactas. After the race he called to announce that he was an idiot for not playing trifectas.

FOURTH RACE
Aqueduct
FEBRUARY 26, 2006

6 FURLONGS. (1.07^{4}) MAIDEN SPECIAL WEIGHT . Purse $41,000 INNER DIRT FOR MAIDENS, THREE YEAR OLDS FOALED IN NEW YORK STATE AND APPROVED BY THE NEW YORK STATE-BRED REGISTRY. Weight, 120 lbs.

Value of Race: $41,000 Winner $24,600; second $8,200; third $4,100; fourth $2,050; fifth $1,230; sixth $137; seventh $137; eighth $137; ninth $137; tenth $137; eleventh $135. Mutuel Pool $391,041.00 Exacta Pool $367,884.00 Quinella Pool $35,161.00 Trifecta Pool $272,741.00

Last Raced	Horse	M/Eqt.	A.	Wt	PP	St	¼	½	Str	Fin	Jockey	Odds $1
	Ferocious Fires	L b	3	120	2	10	1^{hd}	11½	15½	1^{8}	Dominguez R A	2.10
29Jan06 ^{4}Aqu^{2}	Midtown South		3	120	9	1	22½	2^{5}	25½	2^{2}	Coa E M	2.40
8Feb06 ^{2}GP^{7}	Funny Connection	L	3	120	4	5	51½	52½	41½	3¾	Jara F	41.50
2Feb06 ^{6}Aqu^{2}	Tough and Easy	L	3	120	3	8	42½	41½	31½	4¾	Mojica O	4.90
2Feb06 ^{6}Aqu^{7}	Count Town	L	3	120	5	6	8½	61½	6^{6}	55¼	Hill C	125.50
	City Invitation		3	120	1	11	11	11	8½	6^{1}	Arroyo N Jr	18.00
6Jan06 ^{6}Aqu^{6}	Prince o' Pranks	L b	3	120	6	3	3½	3^{hd}	5½	7¾	Luzzi M J	9.00
	New Testament	L b	3	115	11	9	92½	8½	7½	82¼	Kaenel K^{5}	6.70
16Feb06 ^{4}Aqu^{7}	Facial Expression	L bf	3	120	8	2	10^{8}	10½	11	9¾	Garcia Alan	69.00
16Jan06 ^{4}Aqu^{8}	Mygoldenexprssion	L b	3	115	7	4	6^{hd}	7½	94½	105½	Morales P^{5}	88.75
	Exactamento		3	120	10	7	7½	94½	10^{hd}	11	Santos J A	21.90

OFF AT 1:56 Start Good. Won ridden out. Track fast.
TIME :23, :47, :59^{3}, 1:12^{4} (:23.12, :47.08, :59.72, 1:12.91)

$2 Mutuel Prices:

3 – FEROCIOUS FIRES	6.20	3.90	3.20
10 – MIDTOWN SOUTH		3.50	2.70
5 – FUNNY CONNECTION			11.20

$2 EXACTA 3–10 PAID $19.00 $2 QUINELLA 3–10 PAID $12.00
$2 TRIFECTA 3–10–5 PAID $295.00

Ch. c, (May), by Lite the Fuse – Flag On the Gate , by Key to the Flag . Trainer Dutrow Anthony W. Bred by Sanford Goldfarb (NY).

FEROCIOUS FIRES was hustled up along the inside, set the pace from the rail, drew away when asked in upper stretch and was ridden out to the finish. MIDTOWN SOUTH chased the pace from the outside, was no match for the winner and continued on to hold the place. FUNNY CONNECTION was hustled along inside, came wide into the stretch and offered a mild rally outside. TOUGH AND EASY chased the pace along the inside and had no rally. COUNT TOWN raced inside and had no rally. CITY INVITATION broke slowly and raced greenly along the inside. PRINCE O' PRANKS chased the pace from the outside and tired in the stretch. NEW TESTAMENT broke awkwardly, was bothered after the start, raced wide and had no rally. FACIAL EXPRESSION was outrun early, came wide into the stretch and had no rally. MYGOLDENEXPRESSION was finished early. EXACTAMENTO stumbled at the start, raced wide and tired.

Owners– 1, Goldfarb Sanford Davis Ira Glassberg Michael A and Vidro William; 2, Our Canterbury Stables; 3, High Rock Stable Everard Patrick A Everard Elizabeth; 4, Nick-Mike Stables; 5, Jordan Mark T; 6, Willmott Thomas; 7, Geist David W; 8, Candlin John; 9, Gentile Aurelio P Greco Thomas A; 10, La Marca Stable; 11, Playtime Stables

Trainers– 1, Dutrow Anthony W; 2, Levine Bruce N; 3, Ubillo Rodrigo A; 4, O'Brien Leo; 5, Destasio Richard A; 6, Turner William H Jr; 7, Geist David W; 8, Candlin John; 9, Serey Juan; 10, Servis Jason; 11, Reynolds Patrick L

Scratched– Good and Game

$2 Pick Three (3–6–3) Paid $198.50 ; Pick Three Pool $63,591 .

For the same $60, he could have made the obligatory $20 win bet on a 41-1 shot, a $5 trifecta box of Funny Connection and the two favorites, and a pair of $5 straight trifectas with Funny Connection running third behind the two favorites. That would have left him with two winning $5 trifectas, each paying $737.50 for a total return of $1,475 for $60—a 24-1 payoff for emphasizing his correct opinion that Funny Connection probably couldn't beat the two favorites but stood a reasonable chance of beating everyone else.

Superfecta Strategies

The superfecta takes the trifecta one step further, demanding that you come up with the fourth-place finisher as well as the top three. The bet made a brief appearance in American racing during the 1960's and 1970's but fell from favor, first because of a lack of popularity due to its cost and difficulty, and then because it was tainted by race-fixing accusations surrounding the bet at New York harness tracks in the 1970's.

In a typical eight-horse harness race, there are 1,680 (8 x 7 x 6 x 5) possible superfecta combinations. Some race-fixers figured out they could lower their costs and ensure their likelihood of cashing by bribing drivers to hold back two or three horses from finishing fourth or better. Now the crooks only had to box the remaining five (5 x 4 x 3 x 2 = 120) or six (6 x 5 x 4 x 3 = 360) trotters or pacers, and they were guaranteed a profit since the holdbacks included a favorite or two.

The cost issue of the superfecta is in the process of being addressed radically with the recent introduction of 10-cent minimum bets, which are discussed separately below. The importance of this current experiment cannot be overstated, because it actually makes superfectas more affordable than trifectas, has serious implications for the taxation and withholding issues addressed in Chapter 5, and may transform the entire exotic-betting landscape if these lower minimums are extended to other exotic wagers. First, though, let's consider the attractions and drawbacks of the bet at any minimum level.

When deciding whether to extend from a trifecta to a superfecta play, a bettor faces many of the same issues he does when considering whether to step up from an exacta to a trifecta. The difficulty and number of possible outcomes increases by a factor of however many additional horses there are in the field to fill the final slot. You might, for instance, switch from a three-horse exacta box to a 3 x 3 x Something trifecta part-wheel if you have a clever underneath idea like Funny Connection in the example above, or if you're playing against a favorite or two and think you can get them out of the money.

Those decisions become blurry when choosing between a trifecta and superfecta, primarily because we are now talking about the fourth-place finisher in a race, a distant placing less likely to be pinpointed by your handicapping. Also, it's one thing to try to bet against a favorite to win or get him out of the exacta, but significantly more ambitious to decree that he can't even finish fourth.

The whimsy or desire for action that might lead you to try to turn an exacta into a trifecta becomes awfully expensive with an additional slot to fill in the superfecta. A 3 x 3 x 9 trifecta part-wheel costs only $42 (3 x 2 x 7) for $1, but a 3 x 3 x 9 x 9 super-fecta is six times as much at $252 (3 x 2 x 7 x 6). Even if you're willing to spend that much, it is not going to pay six times as much as the trifecta unless something really interesting happens for fourth place. Unless you have a good reason to think that's especially likely, you're back to gambling and hitting the "all" button.

One popular way to play the superfecta is to consider it as a sort of combination of a win selection and a trifecta—keying one horse to win only and then betting on the effective trifecta combinations underneath to provide the 2-3-4 finishers. Keying one horse over three others, for example, costs just $6 at a $1 minimum, but you only have six among thousands of possible combinations. The cost of keying one horse over several others is exactly the same as that for a trifecta box among the same number of "underneath" horses. Keying one horse over four others is $24, over five horses is $60, over six horses is $120, etc.

A variation of this play that makes a superfecta at a $1 minimum more manageable is a trio of double-key part-wheels, where either of your two key horses must win and the other must finish 2-3-4. You could hook up two keys with four other runners for $72 this way:

1,2/1,2/3,4,5,6/3,4,5,6 = 24 bets (2 x 1 x 4 x 3)
1,2/3,4,5,6/1,2/3,4,5,6 = 24 bets (2 x 4 x 1 x 3)
1,2/3,4,5,6/3,4,5,6/1,2 = 24 bets (2 x 4 x 3 x 1)

Adding a fifth underneath horse to this play would increase the cost to $120, and a sixth would make it $180. There will be plenty of frustrating occasions when your two keys both hit the board but fail to win, running 2-3, 2-4, or 3-4, but adding those three permutations would double the cost of the play.

The attraction of the superfecta is the possibility of a very large payout that may be a massive overlay. The cost and difficulty of the superfecta mean that smaller players will be boxing a limited number of choices and fearfully including two or three favorites, while the sheer number of combinations means that some perfectly reasonable outcomes will be overlooked and underbet.

The superfecta is the first bet we have looked at where "pool scooping" becomes a realistic possibility. Pool scooping occurs when there is only a single ticket sold on the winning combination, meaning that one person receives a payoff that may be many times higher than the pure odds would suggest it should be, simply because that particular combination was lost amid the vast number of possibilities.

Here's an example of how that might work. Suppose there is a 12-horse field in a race at a midsized track where the superfecta pool is just $20,000. There are only 20,000 $1 superfecta bets to cover 11,880 possible combinations, and because so many of those 20,000 are duplicative tickets emphasizing the favorites, several hundred or even thousands of the possible superfecta combinations may have only a single winning bet on them. Many others will be uncovered completely, meaning that there will be an "all" payoff—the pool will be shared among those who have the first three finishers. If you had a 1-2-3-4 and 1-2-3-5 and nobody had the correct 1-2-3-6 combination, anyone with a 1-2-3-X ticket would be considered a winner and you would have two winning 1-2-3-all superfectas.

Part of the lure of the superfecta is the chance of receiving a much higher payout than seems warranted by holding the lone winning ticket. It does not take a procession of 50-1 shots for this to happen. In the eighth race at Gulfstream on February 15, 2006, for example, the winner paid $18.40, the 4.70-1 second choice finished second, the 3.40-1 favorite finished third, and a 92-1 shot finished fourth. Even with the two favorites in there, the superfecta should have paid about $16,000 for $1. Only one ticket was sold on the winning combination, however, so after the 25 percent takeout from the pool of $61,877, the lone winning $1 ticket paid $46,407.70, nearly three times what it should have.

(It can work the other way. In the 1999 Breeders' Cup Classic at Gulfstream, the first four finishers were Cat Thief at 19-1, Budroyale at 26-1, Golden Missile at 75-1, and Chester House at 63-1. That computes to a payoff of over $6 million, but because the pool was a mere $923,876, the lone winning $1 ticket returned "only" $692,907 after takeout, though it is unlikely the winner felt too bad about receiving such technically poor value.)

One betting inefficiency that crops up again and again when looking at superfecta payoffs is that a second- rather than third- or fourth-place finish by a longshot frequently leads to a massively overlaid return. This is true with trifectas but even more so with superfectas, where the increasing costs lead many players to use longshots in third and especially fourth positions only. Of the 15 highest superfecta payoffs in the 47 Breeders' Cup races that offered the bet from 1998 through 2004, only six featured a winner at 10-1 or more, but the runner-up was in double digits 13 of those 15 times.

My own forays into the superfecta have been brief and recent. Until 2004, the bet was only offered once a day on New York racing, which accounts for nearly all my handle outside major stakes races. Also, the superfecta was available only on the last race of the day, an event whose outcome I was often already fully invested in because it was the final leg of the pick four or pick six. At this writing, New York now offers two or three superfectas a day on an irregular basis but has yet to adopt the change that would get me far more interested in the bet: the 10-cent minimum.

Dime Supers

Although I have been a noisy proponent of lower minimum bets for some exotic wagers, I claim no authorship of the idea, which other countries implemented decades before U.S. tracks began their current experiment with dime supers. I first ran into them on my honeymoon in London in 1987, when I wandered into a bookmaking shop and found a betting card for a wager called the Heinz 57—so named because it allowed a player to make 57 different parlay bets on one ticket, one for each original variety of Heinz condiments. The minimum bet was just 10 pence per parlay, meaning a player could buy a Heinz ticket for as little as £5.70, which was then worth about $10.

I pretty much forgot about the Heinz until I was stuck for a column one day in 2002 and proposed that the minimum bet for exotic wagers be reduced from $1 to 50 cents. A few fellow exotics players liked the idea, but no one operating a racetrack paid any attention. A year later, I floated the idea again, proposing that the minimum be dropped to a dime. Again there was resounding silence.

A few months later I received a letter postmarked Hinsdale, New Hampshire, with a mutuel ticket inside it:

> "Steve,
>
> We started Dime Supers at Hinsdale today. Since I ripped off the concept from a column you wrote back in July, I bought you the first ticket sold today as a thank you for the idea.
>
> Joe Sullivan III,
> Hinsdale Greyhound Track and OTB"

The ticket read "$0.10 SPRB 1,3,5,7 $2.40"—a 10-cent, four-dog superfecta box, which would have cost $24 at the old $1 minimum but was now available for just $2.40, one-tenth of the normal cost.

A few months later, Sam Houston Race Park in Houston, Texas, became the first Thoroughbred track in America to try dime superfecta boxes, and by the end of 2005, dime supers were available at most major American tracks, with the notable exception of New York.

It remains to be seen whether dime bets will spread beyond the superfecta. Sam Houston has experimented with a 50-cent pick four, and Beulah Park near Cleveland was set to introduce a 25-cent pick six in early 2006.

Reducing the cost of a superfecta by 90 percent obviously brings it within reach of many more bettors and eliminates the bankroll issues that either price out most players altogether or limit many of them to almost hopelessly inadequate investments. At a 10-cent minimum, a six-horse superfecta box or a 4 x 4 x 8 x 8 part-wheel costs $36 instead of $360 and allows average players to make these kinds of investments for the first time. It also allows players to purchase different combinations in different increments and to emphasize certain combinations more heavily than others, which is impractical at a $1 minimum. Someone who makes a six-horse super box for $36 could also go back and key his favored horse over the other five for only an additional $6 instead of the $60 such a key would normally cost.

Only two objections have been raised. First, a few track operators voiced concerns about betting lines being clogged by novices calling out multiple combinations. This may be a plausible argument for not offering dime supers on the handful of big-event days when tracks are actually full, or perhaps offering them only through self-service machines and via wagering accounts. It is a better argument for tracks to install more such betting terminals.

The other people unhappy about dime supers are the big bettors, who fear that their days of pool-scooping and 1-2-3-all payoffs may be over if, at least in theory, 10 times as many combinations are being sold on each race. Such fears are shortsighted. Would these same players like a return to the days of $5 minimum exactas? Dropping that minimum by a factor of five has led to an explosion of exacta pools through greater participation by unsophisticated players. In the long run, the good players will benefit if these pools are made more accessible to everyone.

The current disparity between $1 minimum trifectas and 10-cent minimum superfectas creates some interesting choices for exotics players. Suppose there's a 13-horse race where you were planning to make a four-horse 1-2-3-4 trifecta box for $24. For that same investment, you could instead make this 10-cent superfecta part-wheel:

1,2,3,4/1,2,3,4/1,2,3,4/All = 240 bets (4 x 3 x 2 x 10) @ $0.10 = $24

The $1 superfecta would need to pay 10 times as much as the $1 trifecta for this to work to your advantage. Hitting the "all" button is of course sheer gambling, and you would only want to make this play if you thought there was an unusually good chance of the favorites finishing out of the money. But for $24, there's no law against a little reckless gambling.

4 MULTIRACE EXOTICS

THE DAILY DOUBLE was racing's first exotic wager and remained its only multirace bet long after exactas and trifectas became common. The pick six joined the American betting menu in the early 1980's, but in doing so leapfrogged the double's more logical extensions, the three-race pick three and the four-race pick four. Even now, these multirace bets trail their intrarace equivalents, the trifecta and superfecta, in popularity.

At the 2005 Breeders' Cup Classic, a combined $10.5 million was bet on that race's exacta ($4.48 million), trifecta ($4.22 million), and superfecta ($1.78 million) as opposed to the combined $5.01 million on the double ($1.31 million), pick three ($1.42 million), and pick four ($2.28 million) ending with that race. (Adding in the $4.58 million bet on the pick six brings the totals much closer, but the pick six is really an entirely separate creature without an intrarace equivalent, and despite that impressive pool, it still accounted for under 4 percent of the entire Breeders' Cup Day handle.)

One revealing aspect of those betting totals is a completely opposite hierarchy of popularity within the two types of bets. The two-horse exacta outhandled the three-horse trifecta, which outdistanced the four-horse superfecta. Among the multirace bets, however, the ranking was pick six, pick four, pick three, and double. This trend is likely to increase, given that the pick four is the newest member of the multirace family and the bet showing the strongest current annual growth, while the daily double continues to fade among the multirace bets and survives as a somewhat nostalgic favorite of its aging loyalists.

These numbers and trends speak to some of the fundamental differences between the vertical and horizontal bets. The intraraces are confined to a single race and involve placings behind the winner, while the multiraces require success in consecutive races but involve only picking winners. From the current levels of popularity, it seems that most bettors concentrate on trying to conquer one race at a time and are progressively timid about extending their opinion farther and farther down into that race's order of finish. The multiraces, however, apparently become more appealing the longer they stretch.Virtually all horseplayers dabble in both directions, but most eventually lean one way or the other, though not always for the right reasons. Sometimes the worst thing that can happen to a player is to have some fortuitous success at a particular type of wager early in his career, because he may continue to play that type of bet only because he is trying to re-create that memorable winning moment. Others may find a comfort level with one type of bet and never even consider branching out.

Neither category of bet is inherently superior to the other, but intrarace and multirace wagers tap different skills. The best reason to choose one over the other is to be completely honest with yourself about your strengths and weaknesses as a handicapper. Some of the following distinctions may be useful in making that choice:

1. *Are you a specialist or a generalist?*

All horseplayers have certain favorite types of races—sprints or routes, grass or dirt, graded stakes or bottom-level claimers. It is unusual to find two or three, much less four or six, of your preferred race types being run consecutively on the same card (the notable exception being big-event days when an entire pick six might consist of graded stakes). What you need to ask yourself is whether you are so much stronger on your preferred races that you really should focus your attention and bankroll only on those, playing intrarace exotics in your areas of strength and expertise, or risk compromising your good opinions in some types of races by combining them with your selections in other events where you are weaker.

The ubiquity of full-card simulcasting has made the specialist's lot in life much easier. Someone whose bailiwick is maiden grass races might have only two or three opportunities a week at his home track, but might find five or six such races a day at various tracks around the country. There is nothing wrong with forsaking multirace bets entirely in favor of attacking your area of specialty, one race at a time; in fact, it is a viable blueprint for long-term success.

On the other hand, you don't have to be an expert at every type of race liable to fall into a pick three or pick four in order to succeed at those wagers. Your competition has the same variety of strengths and weaknesses that you do, and being a comprehensive handicapper who is merely competent at all race types puts you ahead of many of your parimutuel opponents—who will be flat-out stabbing or guessing in at least one leg of a multirace bet.

2. *Do you like to do homework the night or morning before the races, or just dive into the upcoming race once you get to the track?*

All intelligent handicapping requires preparation, but you can get away with less of it if you're playing one race at a time instead of three, four, or six of them in advance. There simply isn't enough time to handicap three or more races in the half-hour interval between post times, much less the time to construct a thoughtful multirace play that usually should involve buying multiple tickets.

Playing extended multirace exotics properly really means having a rough draft of your tickets by the time late scratches are announced before the first race of the day. This gives you an invaluable head start on much of your competition and allows you to focus on how late changes, and perhaps track condition, might alter your view of some races.

3. *Is it important to you to see how horses look in the paddock, and how they are being bet, before you wager?*

In multirace betting beyond the daily double, you only get to see the horses and the tote board for the first leg of the wager, and this alone can be a stopper for handicappers who put a great deal of emphasis on equine body language or betting action. Personally, I ignore the former and find the latter essential only when first-time starters are involved. Fortunately, the more enlightened tracks try to accommodate multirace players by positioning firster-loaded maiden races as the first leg of pick fours and pick sixes, and since most tracks offer rolling pick threes, you never have to bet blindly into a race with firsters unless you choose to.

If you're the kind of horseplayer whose best opinions coalesce race by race after looking at the horses and the tote board, multirace betting may not be for you. If, on the other hand, your strengths include being able to predict how races will be bet—knowing before the board opens whether certain horses might be overbet or overlooked—you have an advantage over much of your competition.

4. *Are you playing in a bankroll-appropriate pool?*

Multirace wagers add a wrinkle to the previous discussion of affordability, the same wrinkle that delayed the introduction of pick threes and fours until long after exactas and trifectas were commonplace: Track operators were initially less than enthusiastic about offering these multirace bets because they feared that customers' money would be "tied up" for three or four races, keeping them from churning money on each individual race and thus lowering their overall handle. Such fears have proven to be as foolishly paternalistic and misplaced as the old rationale for $5 minimum exactas, but the short-stacked horseplayer should not be putting all his eggs into multirace baskets.

If your bankroll for a day at the races is $100, you should not be putting $36 into the early pick four, $36 into the pick six, and playing individual races with the remaining $28. Those investments are both too large for your budget and too small for you to be competitive in those pools.

There is also a long-term bankroll issue when considering the more difficult multirace bets, specifically the pick four and pick six. These are bets where even a skilled and well-financed player can go through very long dry spells that can deplete what was supposed to be a seasonal or annual reserve. An exacta or trifecta player can get well in a hurry on a single race, or scale back his action and play more cautiously until he gets his feet back under him. A pick-four or pick-six player doesn't have that option. How many days or weeks are you willing to go 3 for 4 or 5 for 6, handicapping well but running through your bankroll?

5. *Are you better at picking potential winners in many races or at forecasting the extended order of finish in a single race?*

This may seem a variation of the specialist/generalist issue, but it speaks more directly to the different nature of intrarace and multirace bets. There is a crucial difference between being good at coming up with the four or five horses likely to run better than the rest of the field in a given race, as opposed to being good at narrowing those down to the necessarily smaller number of horses with the best chance of finishing first in those races.

Again, this distinction may seem thin: Why isn't a horse who is capable of running second or third in a race just as likely to win it? Technically he *can* win, of course, but the probability of a first-place finish may be much lower than that of hitting the board.

Consider a hypothetical maiden dirt race for 2-year-olds that shapes up as follows, with 80 percent of the action on the three favorites:

- The 6-5 favorite is a second-time starter who ran a Beyer Speed Figure of 75 while finishing second in his debut.
- The 9-5 second choice is a well-bet first-time starter with a precocious pedigree and a trainer who often wins first time out.
- The 5-1 third choice is a horse making his fourth career start and has run three respectable races that earned figures between 60 and 65.
- The rest of the field consists of experienced runners who have never exceeded a figure of 50 and first-time starters with weak credentials who are taking no betting action whatsoever. For the sake of argument, let's say there are no compelling issues of pace, distance, or intriguing longshots to cloud the picture.

Many people will see this as a three-horse race and use all three of the favorites in their multirace wagers, feeling confident they have "locked up" the race by covering the three top horses. They then will watch the race and root for the third choice because he is the biggest price.

The problem with this play is that you have used these three horses in equal strength, as if they have an equal chance of victory. Think about it for a minute, though, and you'll see that they really don't.

The favorite needs only to match his debut to beat the third choice's usual effort. He has already run well enough to win most maiden races, and with any improvement he is a cinch—unless one of the first-timers is something special.

Maybe the second favorite is such a horse. He is the most likely alternative to the favorite to run a figure of 75 or better.

For the third choice to win, however, two things have to happen: The favorite has to regress several lengths, *and* the first-time starter has to be so ordinary that he won't exceed a debut effort that translates to a figure in the mid-60's. Something can and frequently does go wrong in a race, but you need something to go wrong with *both* of these horses for the third choice to have any chance of winning. This is far, far less likely to happen than for just one of the two favorites to do what he is expected to do.

Still, the third choice is very likely to hit the board. He could easily round out an exacta or trifecta under one or both of the favorites. He has to be used under-neath in any intrarace exotic. His chances of winning the race, however, are probably 10 percent or less, making him a terrible underlay at 5-1 and a very poor use of one-third of your multirace investment.

In this example, I would most often use only the two favorites and feel pretty confident about getting through this leg of the multirace sequence. It may seem a small matter to shave the number of horses you use in a given leg of a multirace bet from three to two, but in fact it is a huge difference. It either saves you a third of what you were planning to invest or allows you to use more horses in a different leg of the sequence in a situation where you may actually want a third horse in equal strength or to cast an even wider net. It costs the same amount of money to go 3 x 4 in two legs of a multirace bet as it does to go 2 x 6. Eliminating that third horse in a situation like this will allow you to add a fifth and sixth horse to a race where you may need them, and it is victories by those kinds of horses that send multirace payoffs skyrocketing.

Multirace Cost and Value

Using the same number of horses in every leg of a multirace wager is almost always a bad idea, so the following chart of possible combinations is intended as an illustration of relative costs rather than as a blueprint for actual bets:

No. per race	Double	Pick 3	Pick 4	Pick 6
2	4	8	16	64
3	9	27	81	729
4	16	64	256	4,096
5	25	125	625	15,625

The good news about figuring out the costs and combinations in a multirace wager is that the math is easier. The bad news is that the easier math produces higher costs than intrarace bets that appear to involve the same number of horses. A $1 5 x 5 x 5 trifecta part-wheel is only a $60 bet because we reduce it to 5 x 4 x 3 to eliminate repeating horses in the same race. A $1 5 x 5 x 5 pick-three part-wheel, however, is the full

$125 that simple multiplication would suggest. There's no 1-1 exacta or 1-1-1 trifecta, but there can be a 1-1-1 pick three if number 1 wins all three races.

Before you get too depressed about that seeming 108 percent cost increase, however, remember that you will probably be using fewer horses in each leg of a multirace bet than you will in the bottom slot of a trifecta or superfecta. Even if you don't fully believe the argument that there are certain types of horses much less likely to finish first than second in a race, you would probably concede that a greater number of horses in any race are eligible to finish third or fourth than to win. You will almost certainly find yourself using seven horses as third-place possibilities in a trifecta much more often than going seven-deep in any leg of any multirace wager.

There are 10,000 pick-four combinations in four 10-horse races and only about half as many superfectas (10 x 9 x 8 x 7 = 5,040) in a 10-horse field. But while such a superfecta will sometimes pay with an "all" in the final position, pick fours almost never go unhit. Picking the winner of a fourth race is a lot easier than picking a fourth-place finisher.

In Chapter 2, we used the example of two five-horse races in a daily double to illustrate the inherent value of a multirace bet in reducing the effective takeout in parimutuel wagering. A pair of $6 winners will usually yield a daily double paying more than the $18 parlay because those $6 mutuels have each been taxed at 15 percent, while together they have been taxed just once at 20 percent. This value continues and grows with additional legs of a pick three, four, or six even though the overall takeout rate frequently rises to 25 percent on these true exotics. A 25 percent takeout on a four-race bet means an effective takeout of only 6.25 percent per race, and a pick six cuts it to 4.17 percent.

Sticking with winning 2-1 shots, let's see how this works in theory. A horse who is exactly 2-1 has 28.33 percent of the money bet on him in a jurisdiction where the WPS takeout is 15 percent. A daily double of two such horses will, if bet in the same proportions as the win pool, account for 8.03 percent (28.33 percent x 28.33 percent) of the daily-double pool, producing a payout of $19.80 under a 20 percent takeout—a 10 percent "bonus" on the $18 parlay price.

A third such 2-1 winner in a pick-three sequence will mean a winning pick three with 2.27 percent of the pool. Even after a 25 percent takeout, the $2 payoff is $65.80, better than a 20 percent improvement on the $54 parlay. A fourth such winner in a pick four would lead to a payoff of $232, more than 40 percent over the parlay price of $162.

At least it would in theory, and often does in practice, but less so when there is a succession of 2-1 winners. The overbetting of favorite-laden combinations that we saw in intrarace pools is amplified in multirace pools. The same short-bankroll issues are part of it, and there is an even greater reluctance by most players to pitch a favorite from a multirace than an intrarace bet. If you toss a favorite from an exacta and he beats you, you may simply shrug and turn the page to the next race. Players seem more reluctant to jeopardize a three-race sequence with such an elimination, living in fear of something interesting happening in the first two legs and then not being alive to the favorite in the third leg. So they include the favorite as one of their two or three horses in each leg, overbetting the most obvious combinations and simultaneously depriving themselves of more likely and lucrative outcomes.

The most common pick-three and pick-four investments are $1 part-wheels using two, three, or four horses per race, totaling between $25 and $100, and leaning on the favorites. Such tickets may simply be the most logical outgrowth of how players think they should be attacking these wagers—take the most-likely winners with the most-likely winners with the most-likely winners, and hope for the best. This is simply a ruinous approach to these bets, though a source of opportunity for those who play them more thoughtfully.

Let's look at the probabilities and payoffs for those who still think the best way to play a pick three is to make a part-wheel of your "top picks" in each race. A 3 x 3 x 3 pick-three play requires $27 bet for each $1 unit. How likely is it to come in, and what does it pay when it does?

Roughly speaking, one of the three favorites wins any given race 60 percent of the time. This may lead you to believe you're more likely to win than lose such a pick-three play, but you have to multiply 60 percent by 60 percent by 60 percent to find your true chances of winning all three legs. That works out to just a 21.6 percent strike rate. If you're only going to collect 21.6 percent of the time on a $27 investment, each time you win, you need your winning pick threes to pay an average of $125 for $1 (usually posted as a $250 for $2 payoff) just to break even. The average pick-three combining one of the three favorites in each leg pays far less.

No one would play the races by making win bets on the three favorites in every race—you would collect 60 percent of the time, but you would need an average $10 win mutuel to break even. Everyone grasps that the average win mutuel for one of the three favorites is far less than $10. Yet people continue to play the pick three in exactly the same fashion, as if doing this in a separate pool will somehow make an ill-advised bet a winning one. Being "right" three times in a row does not necessarily make you a winner.

Using the same number of horses in each leg of a multirace bet cannot possibly be an optimal approach. You are not only assigning each of your horses an identical chance of victory, an unlikely assessment three straight times, but also saying that there's no race in the sequence that really requires only one or two horses. For about the same $27 you might spend on a 3 x 3 x 3 part-wheel, look at some of the other permutations you could play that would more accurately reflect the differences in various races:

    1 x 3 x 9 = $27
    1 x 5 x 5 = $25
    2 x 2 x 7 = $28
    2 x 3 x 5 = $30

Note that these are not necessarily recommended plays. A 1 x 5 x 5 part-wheel might be advisable only in the rare cases where you can find no better way to play your "single" than to dilute him by a factor of 25, and if you thought you were getting proper value by going five-deep in two consecutive races. The point is to avoid the expensive, inflexible, and inefficient 3 x 3 x 3 part-wheel so many of your lazy competitors are making.

The ABC's (and X's) of Multirace Betting

There are all sorts of ways to rate or rank horses when handicapping a race, ranging from using simple checkmarks and crossouts to constructing a mathematically correct fair-odds betting line on the entire race. Each horseplayer must arrive at his own method, one that reflects both his particular handicapping methods and the amount of time and precision he wants to invest in the endeavor.

You must, however, have a method of some kind that forces you to consider, evaluate, and finally decide what to do with every horse in a race. My own such method has evolved over the years to a letter-grade system that ultimately determines the mechanics of my multirace wagers. I rank each horse in a race, in descending order of appeal, as an A, B, C, or X, and construct my tickets accordingly.

It's not quite that simple. There are at least two stages to the grading process—a preliminary assessment of the race, then a fine-tuning that incorporates value and strategic considerations. Between those stages, a horse who began as a B may well descend to a C or even an X rating. Also, like any waffling teacher grading papers, I often end up adding pluses or minuses to the ratings as a final separator. In the broadest sense, though, here are the characteristics of each tier of horses:

A Horses: Primary contenders, likely winners, or horses who are going to offer spectacular betting value, such as a horse you think will be 20-1 but actually has a 20 percent chance to win. Usually there will be from one to three A's in a race. In some cases, an initial A horse may be one that you will ultimately bet against, even strongly, solely because of his actual or anticipated price, but that is a later decision.

B Horses: Reasonable contenders, next most likely to win if the A's fail but less deserving of emphasis for reasons of ability, value, or both. B's often become C's in final refinements.

C Horses: Unlikely winners who can't be entirely eliminated and who may warrant minor inclusion on at least some tickets, depending on how the other races in a multirace sequence shape up. I usually end up further refining C's into three subcategories: C+'s, who I definitely want to use in some minor way, usually because of their price; C-'s, who ultimately merit only the tiniest, most defensive inclusion; and Cx's, horses I acknowledge can win but finally decide I will allow to beat me, effectively downgrading them to X's.

X Horses: Eliminations, horses who lack the ability to be competitive to win, are clearly running on the wrong surface or distance, and/or figure to be completely compromised by the way a race will be run. An X horse might be a perfectly reasonable inclusion on the bottom of a trifecta or superfecta ticket, but so many things would have to go wrong in a race for him to finish first that he is an unwise inclusion to win.

I cannot emphasize strongly enough that these grades involve first-place finishes only and have no application to intrarace wagering. I do not play my A's over my B's in exactas or construct A/B,B/B,B,C,C,C trifecta part-wheels. My grades speak only to prospects of outright victory, and incorporate three broad factors: likelihood of winning, value relative to likely odds, and strategic ticket-construction decisions.

Let's examine each of those three elements, returning to the hypothetical maiden race discussed above, assigning the nine horses fictitious names that reflect their broad credentials, and my preliminary grades:

1 Bold Debut	**A**
2 Hot Firster	**AB**

3 Old Reliable	BC
4 Jockey Switch	C
5 Obscure Firster	C
6 Dreadful Firster	X
7 No Ability	X

Bold Debut, whom we regard as close to a cinch unless Hot Firster is indeed a sizzler, is the simplest sort of an A. He is the likeliest winner and there are no knocks on him. Hot Firster is the one to fear, and one of the crucial questions we will have to decide in Step 2 is whether to give him equal prominence on our tickets with Bold Debut or to create a separate B tier for him.

Old Reliable is the third most likely winner of the race and we can't draw an X through him, at least not yet. He's clearly not an A, and the question of whether he's a B, C, or X will be based on value and strategy, not on simple ability.

Jockey Switch is the kind of horse you can't draw a line through on the first pass. We have given him his name because we're supposing that after two dull performances under identical conditions, today he is switching from a 10-pound apprentice to one of the top five riders at the track. We could have just as easily named him Just Claimed, Off Slowly Last, or Equipment Change. The point is that he's the kind of horse that has something a little different or interesting happening today, which means we can't eliminate him until we take a closer second look.

We'll also wait and see on Obscure Firster, a debut runner who is highly unlikely to be as good as either Bold Debut or Hot Firster but has no strong negatives among his connections, workouts, or pedigree. If the race falls apart and the favorites fail, he might be good enough to win by default.

It's not too soon to draw an X through Dreadful Firster, who comes from a trainer who is 0 for 62 with debut runners over the last five years, has been working slowly and infrequently, and is being ridden by an exercise rider who rarely gets mounts in races. No Ability also gets an X off five starts in which he has been trounced by lesser fields of this kind while showing no improvement whatsoever.

So we're left with five open horses after Round 1 of assessment. Some bettors, bless them, would stop at this point and use all five of them in equal strength in a double or pick three, maybe even in a pick four or pick six if they have a great deal more money than common sense. Such a play is obviously highly inefficient because you are devoting 80 percent of your investment to beating Bold Debut, a horse we think is 50 percent or better to win the race, while allotting the same amount of money to both Bold Debut and Jockey Switch, a horse we have kept eligible by the slender thread of a single positive factor.

Further thought, research, and refinement might cause the following change of grades. We might decide to keep Bold Debut as an A but make Hot Firster a B because we think that the mistake the public will make in betting the race is to undervalue the quality of Bold Debut's performance. We might then decide that the chances of a misfire by both favorites is sufficiently slim that we should downgrade Old Reliable from a B to a very defensive C, which is where we'll also leave Obscure Firster.

What you do with Jockey Switch will be a factor of your own handicapping methods. I personally would almost never spend money on a horse because of a change in riders alone, without some corroborating evidence that vastly improved performance was coming today. These are some of the toughest decisions in handicapping, and my general opinion is that horseplayers usually make too much of individual change factors and overbet them. Just because you are smart enough to notice something different today, it does not compel you to spend money on a horse.

So we'll let Jockey Switch beat us, leaving us with one A, one B, and two somewhat weak C's. Now what? It all depends on what pool we're playing and what the other races look like. Almost every possible answer to what to do with these selections, however, involves the same key strategy: The one thing we won't be doing is buying a single ticket that uses all four of them—at least not on the same ticket. In fact, much of the remaining discussion of multirace wagering will have buying multiple tickets as its guiding principle.

Double and Pick-Three Tickets

Suppose that the maiden race we have been discussing was the first half of a daily double that concludes with another race in which we have two A's and two B's. The easiest and worst way to play this double would be to buy a single 4 x 4 $2 double part-wheel of 1,2,3,4/1,2,3,4 for $32. That would cover every combination of the four potential winners in each race but would give no emphasis to our preferred horses in either leg. We would have the same $2 on both the 1/1 and 1/2 combinations of Bold Debut with our two A's in the second race as we do on the 3/3 and 3/4 combinations of Old Reliable with our two B's in the second race.

We could begin to structure this play better by giving different strength to our three tiers of horses in the maiden race and instead make three part-wheels, spending the same $32 as follows:

$4 daily double 1/1,2,3,4	= 1 x 4 x $4 = $16
$2 daily double 2/1,2,3,4	= 1 x 4 x $2 = $ 8
$1 daily double 3,4/1,2,3,4	= 2 x 4 x $1 = $ 8
Total	= $32

This could be further refined to give slightly greater emphasis to our two second-race A's this way:

$5 daily double 1/1,2	= 1 x 2 x $5 = $10
$3 daily double 1/3,4	= 1 x 2 x $3 = $ 6
$3 daily double 2/1,2	= 1 x 2 x $3 = $ 6
$1 daily double 2/3,4	= 1 x 2 x $1 = $ 2
$1 daily double 3,4/1,2,3,4	= 2 x 4 x $1 = $ 8
Total	= $32

Instead of having the same $2 on each of the 16 possibilities, you now have emphasized your positive opinions as follows:

A/A @ $5
A/B @ $3
B/A @ $3

In exchange, you are decreasing the B/B, C/A, and C/B combinations from $2 to $1. If we were investing on a grander scale than $32, or if bets were allowed in 50-cent increments, we could have gone one step further and played the C/A combos a little heavier than the C/B ones.

In a daily double, though, doing so much spreading is rarely a good idea. In this example, I would be far less likely to play all 32 of these combinations than to make a pair of $16 doubles of Bold Debut to my two second-race A's and leave it at that. In longer-sequence bets with potentially high payouts, there's something to be said for getting through races just to stay alive, but in a double, you really want to press and maximize your opinions.

Let's say that the two second-race A's are 3-1 and 5-1. If the doubles to them from Bold Debut are paying $25 and $35, I can triple their win prices by betting those two doubles and I haven't tripled my risk because I believe Bold Debut is at least 50 percent to win.

The double is a bit of a relic, and between its simplicity and the double-edged sword of being able to see prospective payouts during the betting—double-edged because (a) it's nice to know, but (b) plenty of tote-watchers will pounce on any inefficiently bet combinations—there are few intrinsic advantages to playing a double beyond the conceptual takeout reduction of betting two opinions at a cut rate.

One situation in which the double can be an effective tool is when one race features a seemingly unbeatable odds-on favorite and you have almost any kind of an opinion in the other leg. In the Whirlaway Stakes at Aqueduct on February 11, 2006, Achilles of Troy was a virtual cinch, a legitimate stakes horse running against five unaccomplished opponents who were simply 8 to 10 lengths slower on paper. I would almost entertain an argument that he was a reasonable win bet at odds of 3-10, but of course I was determined to try to improve that price.

Many bettors will simply pass such a race instead of bothering to bet at $2.60, but the question they should be asking is whether there is a way to improve that price. Unfortunately, I had absolutely no good "underneath" opinions in the Whirlaway, so intrarace betting was not an option, but I did have a small idea about the finale on the card. I wasn't crazy about the 8-5 favorite and saw only three plausible alternatives, so I pitched the favorite and made three $100 doubles: Achilles of Troy to Johnie By Night, Token Dem, and Gin Societe.

Here were the possible payoffs for the double, posted after the Whirlaway. Next to each double price is the win price for each horse:

Horse	DD Willpay	$2 Win Willpay
1 Cooking the Books	$ 96.50	$82.50
2 Cat's Lad	$ 63.50	$43.00
3 Rodeo Runner	$ 33.40	$24.20
4 Phantom G	$ 33.80	$23.20
5 Johnie By Night	$ 18.00	$12.00
6 Whilstone	$ 41.80	$35.00
7 Token Dem	$ 22.00	$12.60
8 Gin Societe	$ 82.50	$63.50
9 Malibu Move	$ 7.70	$ 5.20
10 Boggy Creek D.	$100.50	$49.80
11 Speedjama	$ 33.20	$21.00

Johnie By Night won, getting me back $900 for the $300 investment, a lot better than the $390 I would have collected with a win bet on Achilles of Troy. (Yes, I could and should have bet the three doubles in different amounts for a more equalized return and done better, but it was one of those last-minute ideas.)

The interesting part of the payoffs above is that Achilles of Troy was worth more than $2.60 in most of them. Even if you loved Malibu Move, you could have gotten nearly a 50 percent premium on him by playing the $7.70 double rather than the $5.20 win bet.

An even better bonus was available to those who played the

pick three on Races 7 through 9. The race preceding the Whirlaway, an allowance event for older horses, featured two favorites—Manchurian at 7-5 and Liquor Cabinet at 3-1—who towered over the field. (Three weeks later, they would return to run 1-2 in the Stymie Handicap.) Liquor Cabinet won at $8.20, and the pick three combining him with Achilles of Troy ($2.60) and Johnie By Night ($12) paid $75. For the same $300 invest-ment I made in the double, I could have made a $50 2 x 1 x 3 pick-three part-wheel and gotten back $1,875 instead of $900.

The idea of hitting a $75 pick three doesn't get anyone's pulse racing, but if you only need to spend $12 to hit it, it's the same as betting a $12.50 winner on the nose. There's nothing wrong with sextupling your money for what amounts to having three pretty unremarkable opinions—liking two favorites, one cinch, and ducking one favorite.

In a double, as discussed previously, there's no point in getting involved if you don't have two opinions worth betting and combining. You need an angle or an idea for both races. As you move to the pick three and beyond, however, it is possible and profitable to get involved even if you are feeling less than inspired about one event. One of the mistakes that almost everyone makes is in thinking he needs to be clever or contrary in every single race of a multirace sequence. A pick three may well make sense even if in one leg, you're going to use the same three favorites that most tickets will. You don't want to do that three times in a row, but if you have good ideas in two of the three races, you don't really hurt yourself by just getting through the third.

In that Liquor Cabinet-Manchurian allowance race, for example, let's say that you liked not only those two favorites but also a third horse, 9-2 third choice Golden Man. Had you used all three of them in equal strength in a 3 x 1 x 3 pick-three part-wheel and then watched Manchurian win at odds of 7-5, you might have felt crestfallen—you went three-deep and got a lousy $4.90 winner. That's emotionally understandable, but mathematically unduly harsh.

If Manchurian attracted about the same percentage of pick-three action as he did in the win pool, he had 34.7 percent of all pick-three tickets sold. You had him on 33.3 percent of your combinations. Big deal. You didn't advance your position but, bad a result for you as it might seem, you didn't weaken yourself either. You held your ground, in effect, and would still have capitalized if the rest of your play was correct.

This concept is most important in the pick four and pick six, where there is frequently a five- or six-digit payout despite one or two winning favorites in a sequence, but the same principle is true in the pick three. It may help to clarify the idea by considering how often favorites will win in any given three-race sequence. Since favorites win roughly one-third of all races, it's pretty easy to see how often either zero, one, two, or three favorites are likely to come in—and the results may surprise you:

0 favorites:	2/3 x 2/3 x 2/3	= 8/27
1 favorite:	1/3 x 2/3 x 2/3	= 4/27
	2/3 x 1/3 x 2/3	= 4/27
	2/3 x 2/3 x 1/3	= 4/27
Total:		= 12/27
2 favorites:	1/3 x 1/3 x 2/3	= 2/27
	1/3 x 2/3 x 1/3	= 2/27
	2/3 x 1/3 x 1/3	= 2/27
Total		= 6/27
3 favorites	1/3 x 1/3 x 1/3	= 1/27

The surprising part may be that any random three-race sequence is eight times as likely to include no winning favorites as three winning favorites. The flip side of this is that 19 out of 27 times, there is at least one winning favorite in a pick-three sequence.

This nugget should reinforce two points: first, that it is folly to play wide-net tickets like a 4 x 4 x 4 pick-three part wheel without emphasizing favorites you like, and second, that you shouldn't duck a pick three altogether just because you think there is a solid favorite in one or two legs.

What if there's a sequence where there are three consecutive standouts? Some bettors will try to crush such combinations with a single punch on the three favorites, but remember that even if you believe each horse stands a 50 percent chance of winning, there is still only a 1 in 8 chance that all three of them will win (1/2 x 1/2 x 1/2). It is three times likelier that two of them will win and a third will lose. Rather than splitting hairs and trying to isolate which of the three races will see the favorite go down, there is another approach that becomes even more useful in pick fours and pick sixes—making multiple tickets involving "main" and "backup" horses, a method that dovetails with an A-B-C-X grading system.

Suppose there's a three-race sequence in which you think there is a standout in every race and you have two secondary choices in each leg—in effect, one A and two C's in each race. Rather than making a 1 x 1 x 1 cold punch, or spreading out with 27 same-sized bets by making a 3 x 3 x 3 part-wheel and rooting against your top pick in each race, you might make the following three part-wheels:

A/A/A,C,C = 3 bets
A/A,C,C/A = 3 bets
A,C,C/A/A = 3 bets

Of your nine bets, three are the same A-A-A combination, and you'll make a decent profit if all the favorites win. Your six other bets are all the possible permutations of two of your standouts winning and one of them losing to your next two choices. You didn't have to decide which race was going to feature the losing favorite, and you're covered if any two of your three standouts win. Instead of buying 27 combinations to get there, you have bought only nine.

Both the double and the pick three are bets best played by narrowing your scope and trying to maximize the value of your opinion. They are not bets that should be played simply to "have" it regardless of the cost or number of combinations it takes to get there. There is no point in playing a double if you're clueless in one leg—we're just back to making win bets at a higher takeout that way. While you can afford one neutral or nonamplifying result in a pick three, again it is a bet you shouldn't be playing if you only have an opinion in one of the three races.

This paradigm begins to change as we move farther out in the solar system of multirace exotics.

Pick-Four Tickets

The pick four is the fastest-growing wager in American racing today. It began appearing more than a decade after the pick six was launched in the United States in the early 1980's, and in my opinion it has become so popular because it provides a far more accessible version of the pick six. With a $1 rather than $2 minimum, and two fewer races in the sequence, the pick four offers a vastly more affordable opportunity to play an extended multirace bet with the feel of a daily tournament and a perpetual possibility of gigantic payouts for coming up with winners rather than fourth-place finishers.

At the $1 minimum, a 2 x 3 x 2 x 3 pick-four part-wheel costs only $36, while a 2 x 3 x 2 x 3 x 2 x 3 pick-six play costs $432 at the usual $2 minimum. Many guppies still make $36 pick-six investments—about all you can get for $36 is a 1 x 1 x 1 x 2 x 3 x 3 part-wheel, less than a fig leaf's worth of coverage against heavily armed competition—but most players have figured out that they stand a much better chance of ever collecting a four- or five-digit payoff on a similar investment by instead playing the pick four.

The fourth leg makes a pick four one level tougher and more rewarding than a pick three, but also takes the entire proposition into new strategic territory. Only the most heavily bankrolled players will try to crush a limited number of combinations. In general, dollars are better allocated to using additional horses that will send payoffs skyrocketing rather than repeating low-paying tickets.

The possibility of significantly overlaid payoffs is much higher than in a pick three, where all 512 combinations in three eight-horse fields are sure to be covered and in roughly the "correct" proportions relative to win prices. Adding a fourth eight-horse field takes that universe of possible outcomes up to 4,096 combinations.

The single biggest mistake that most pick-four players make may be in trying to hit it with the same level of investment they put into a pick three. The $24 or $36 or $48 that players invest in pick-three part-wheels buys surprisingly less coverage in a pick four.

Consider the difference between a 3 x 3 x 4 pick-three part-wheel and what the same $36 will buy you in a similar pick-four play—a 3 x 3 x 2 x 2 part-wheel. Instead of having one race where you have four horses, you now must get through two separate races with only half as much coverage. Putting aside the odds and merits of the individual horses, you've gone from having four of eight horses, a 50 percent chance, to having to get by with just two of eight horses and doing it twice—a 1 in 16 chance.

Playing the pick four with an inadequate bankroll is worse than never playing the bet at all. This is not a recommendation for prospective players to start betting over their heads and comfort levels, but to consider allocating a larger share of their day's investment to the bet than they would to their standard unit of play for an exacta box or pick-three part-wheel. Instead of putting $24 into three different pick threes on the card, consider putting $72 into the pick four. Or, rather than putting $36 into the pick four three times a week, play only on Saturdays and spend $108.

Spending more money is only part of the solution. Opening your wallet to buy a 3 x 3 x 4 x 4 part-wheel gives you more coverage but is not the best way to spend $144, for the same reason that this kind of crude part-wheel rarely is in any pool—you are giving equal weight and strength to every horse on your ticket, and overspending on simpler races while depriving yourself of the opportunity to catch the messy long-shot in the wide-open race that will make the payoff attractive.

The pick four lends itself particularly well to a multi-ticket approach with tiered horses. Just as in the early days of the pick six, when only a few players had figured out that going two- or three-deep in every race on one ticket was not an optimal strategy, simply making out multiple tickets will give you a big leg up on the competition in the pick four these days. The most successful current pick-four players I know are pick-six players who have adapted some of the complex multi-ticket strategies for their bet to its smaller, four-legged cousin.

My usual pick-four investment is somewhere between $100 and $500, and I do not recall having ever played the bet with a single ticket. A more common play for me involves putting in between five and 10 tickets, as I did while spending $192 on an uninspiring-looking sequence at Aqueduct on November 19, 2005.

The chart below illustrates how I had handicapped the sixth through ninth races on that day's card. Each horizontal line shows how I had graded each horse in the sequence:

Race	A Horses	B Horses	C Horses	X Horses
6th	3,7	2,8	1,4,9,10	—
7th	1,14	—	3,15	2,7,8,9
8th	1,8	4,7	—	3,6,9,10
9th	5,9	—	2,8	1,3,4,6,7,10

If I had combined all of my "open" horses on a single ticket, it would have been an 8 x 4 x 4 x 4 part-wheel for $512. If I had shaved my C horses out of the play, I would have been left with a 4 x 2 x 4 x 2 part-wheel for $64 that would have eliminated every horse in the sequence who was over 10-1, and would have left me with no more than a $1 ticket even if all my A horses had won. This latter play is what the majority of low and midlevel players will end up doing.

So what I did instead was my standard mix-and-match array, which usually dictates the following. To win, I must get home either four A's; three A's and one B; two A's and two B's; or three A's and one C. Here was how those tickets worked out:

Ticket	Array	Details	Combos/Unit	Cost
1	AAAA	3,7/1,14/1,8/5,9	16 @ $4	= $64
2	BAAA	2,8/1,14/1,8/5,9	16 @ $2	= $32
3	AABA	3,7/1,14/4,7/5,9	16 @ $2	= $32
4	BABA	2,8/1,14/4,7/5,9	16 @ $1	= $16
5	CAAA	1,4,9,10/1,14/1,8/5,9	32 @ $1	= $32
6	ACAA	3,7/3,15/1,8/5,9	16 @ $1	= $16
7	AAAC	3,7/1,14/1,8/2,8	16 @ $1	= $16
			TOTAL	= $208

I have not chosen this example to illustrate my astute handicapping or a significant score. Obviously I did not exactly have brilliant insights into the opening leg, since I used all eight starters and got an A home as the 3-1 second choice. In the next leg my A's ran 1-2 but with the uninteresting 5-2 second choice edging the 6-1 "smart" selection and with me neglecting to bet the $43.60 exacta. When a third A won the eighth race as the 2-1 favorite, I was hardly thrilled about my pick-four prospects.

But at least I was alive for $4 instead of $1 to my two A's, and alive for $1 tickets to my two C's, a pair of iffy longshots whom I might have discarded if I were playing a single ticket and trying to whittle it down from $512. Despite having two second choices and a favorite win the first three legs, the prospective $2 payoffs and my potential returns for $208 were not terrible:

5(A): $ 394 @ $4 = $ 788
9(A): $ 308 @ $4 = $ 616
2(C): $2,810 @ $1 = $ 1,405
8(C): $3,162 @ $1 = $ 1,581

Good old number 8, Intergalactic, came though at 22-1, the best outcome and nearly a 7-1 return on my investment for a sequence of races where I hardly had stellar opinions.

Calling or punching out seven different tickets on a $208 investment may seem like a lot of fuss, but I am convinced that this little bit of extra effort produces a huge advantage. Even if you make out only three tickets rather than one, giving yourself some backup horses in two of the four races with your main selections in the other, this will give you opportunities unavailable to those whittling themselves out of horses like Intergalactic on a single ticket.

What I really did by making out an array of seven tickets was say that if I could be "right" about my A preferences in any three of the four races, I could be "wrong" and have a C win any individual race. By playing a single ticket, I would have had to make the specific choice that the ninth race was the precise one where I wanted to spread out, rather than having different options.

Some people might argue that I turned a 22-1 winner into a 7-1 return, but the truth is that I hardly "picked" Intergalactic to win. He was my fourth choice in a race where the two favorites looked perfectly solid. If I had liked him enough to designate him as an A, I would have had a $4 pick four for a $6,324 return, and if I had liked him enough to make him a B, I would have had a $2 ticket for a $3,162 rather than $1,581 return. I got about what my opinion deserved, and probably a bit more.

In this example, the horse that made the pick four worthwhile came in the last race of the sequence. Had Intergalactic's triumph come one race earlier, I would have been in a position to take advantage of an opportunity that pick-four and pick-six players should always be aware of, one that does not require you to complete a winning sequence to benefit from a good earlier result.

Eight days after the Intergalactic race, it was Holidayfest at Aqueduct, a Saturday-after-Thanksgiving card featuring the

Demoiselle, Remsen, and Cigar Mile. As we will discuss at greater length in Chapter 7, these big-event cards present some of racing's best exotic-betting opportunities because they attract far more uninformed and poorly conceived bets than your usual rainy weekday card.

The three stakes races were the first three legs of the pick four and I was eager to combine my essential opinions, which were that Bluegrass Cat was a cinch in the Remsen (the seventh race) but that the Demoiselle (sixth) and Cigar (eighth) were wide-open contests with vulnerable favorites ripe for upsets. The final race of the day, and the sequence, was an uninspiring statebred allowance race.

My little pick-four chart looked like this:

Race	A Horses	B Horses	C Horses	X Horses
6th	2,4,5	—	1,3	—
7th	1	—	4,5	2,3,6,7,8
8th	5,8,9	7,10,11	—	1,2,3,4,6
9th	1,11	7,8	9,10	3,6

These opinions produced the following tickets:

Ticket	Array	Details	Combos/Unit	Cost
1	AAAA	2,4,5/1/5,8,9/1,11	18 @ $5	= $90
2	AABA	2,4,5/1/7,10,11/1,11	18 @ $3	= $54
3	AAAB	2,4,5/1/5,8,9/7,8	18 @ $3	= $54
4	AABB	2,4,5/1/7,10,11/7,8	18 @ $2	= $36
5	CAAA	1,3/1/5,8,9/1,11	12 @ $1	= $12
6	AAAC	2,4,5/1/5,8,9/9,10	18 @ $1	= $18
			TOTAL	= $264

(Please note that I am not suggesting you need $264 to play the pick four. In this example, had you bought $2 rather than $3 or $5 units on the first three tickets and $1 units on the others, the same combinations could have been covered for $156.)

Things could not have started out better. In the first leg, number 2, Wonder Lady Anne, was an easy winner of the Demoiselle at $23.40, then number 1, Bluegrass Cat, led all the way as the 3-5 Remsen favorite. Five of my six tickets were still alive, the ones ending AA, BA, AB, BB, and even AC. Unless an X horse won, the only thing that could beat me was a B in the Cigar and a C in the finale.

I wasn't too upset when the first half of that latter scenario came true in the Cigar, because the B who won was Purge at $53, leaving me alive to my two A's and two B's:

1(A): $ 7,266 @ $3 = $10,899
11(A): $ 9,554 @ $3 = $14,331
7(B): $16,531 @ $2 = $16,531
8(B): $10,814 @ $2 = $10,814

At this point I had half the field covered in an eight-horse race to get back a minimum profit of over $10,000. I felt like I had the right four horses and was about 80 percent to prevail, but if I just sat still I could still get nothing. If someone had offered to buy my live tickets for $8,000, I would have taken it in a heartbeat. No such exchange is available at the track, but in a situation like this you can make one by betting against yourself. Financial investors do it all the time under the headings of hedging and arbitrage.

The four horses who could ruin my day were going off at 7-1, 12-1, 15-1, and 35-1. The two C's I was no longer alive to were the shortest and longest of those. I was sick enough about not being alive to 35-1 Casper Peterson, one of my C's, since that pick four was paying just over $51,000. I would have been alive for $1 to that one had I made Purge an A instead of a B, but unfortunately there's no cashing window for "if."

There was no way to guarantee myself a $10,000 return regardless of the outcome of the race without making an additional $3,000 in win bets, but I didn't want to get spooked by Casper and wanted to ensure some meaningful return in any case. So I put in $1,000 in hedge bets, taking $200 on Casper and my two X's and $400 on the 7-1 C horse I was no longer alive to. I had increased my cost basis from $264, the initial pick-four investment, to $1,264 for the whole mess, but compare the before-and-after scenarios of investment and return:

Without Hedging:
1: $264/$10,899 = +$10,635
3: $264/$0   =   -$264
6: $264/$0   =   -$264
7: $264/$16,531 = +$16,267
8: $264/$10,814 = +$10,550
9: $264/$0   =   -$264
10: $264/$0   =   -$264
11: $264/$14,331 = +$14,067

After Hedging:
1: $1,264/$10,899 = +$ 9,635
3: $1,264/$6,350 = +$ 5,086
6: $1,264/$2,620 = +$ 1,356
7: $1,264/$16,531 = +$15,267
8: $1,264/$10,814 = +$ 9,550
9: $1,264/$3,560 = +$ 2,296
10: $1,264/$7,350 = +$ 6,086
11: $1,264/$14,331 = +$13,067

As you've probably guessed by now, Casper Peterson rocketed to the front, held off my live-pick-four pursuers down the stretch, and paid $73.50 to win. The $200 win bet took the sting out of missing the quartet of five-digit pick fours—and probably reduced the amount of time I spent kicking myself for not having made Purge an A instead of a B.

Despite such occasional frustrations, the pick four has joined the pick six as my favorite way to bet. As will be discussed in Chapter 6, the pick six is at its most attractive when there is a carryover, which happens only once or twice a week in New York. Making the pick six the focus of your everyday playing means not only investing in non-carryovers but also enduring roller-coaster bankroll swings because of the infrequent strike rate even the best players can expect. The pick four offers a mini-tournament once or twice a day, with a lower entry fee and a higher chance of more frequent success.

5 THE TAXMAN COMETH

SOMETIMES HAVING PARTNERS is a good idea when you're playing the races. Four friends who each want to spend $32 on a pick four, or especially a pick six, would do better by pooling their $128 than going it alone with short money. Some bigger players have been known to sell a percentage of their tickets (usually at a markup) to passive investors who want some action without doing any handicapping, as a way of lessening their risk or gaining additional capital.

Suppose you had a partner, though, who didn't put up any money, didn't pay for any losses, but demanded 25 percent of your very best payoffs? In addition to being unfair, it could bankrupt you before the end of the year. One of the downsides of exotic betting is that when you finally hit something big, you will discover that you have precisely such a partner. His name is Uncle Sam.

In the hedging story at the end of the previous chapter, I wrote that my $200 win saver on Casper Peterson, good for a

$7,350 return, was decent consolation for missing a couple of pick-four payoffs in the $10,000 range. From a cash-flow perspective, it was actually a virtually identical result: Under the absurd gambling regulations of the Internal Revenue Service, a $10,000 pick-four score is subject to a 25 percent federal-income-tax withholding, meaning you will receive only $7,500. A $7,350 triumph in the win pool, however, goes unreported and untaxed.

The current tax code is unfair to all gamblers, but singles out racing's exotic bettors for particularly brutal treatment. That these regulations have not been changed even as the exotics have come to dominate modern racetrack betting is an ongoing disgrace for the American racing industry, which has shown little interest or initiative in working to change them even though tracks would benefit as much as their customers. While most seasoned exotics players have reluctantly and bitterly accepted them as a cost of doing business, they can create financial complications for the most law-abiding citizen and are serious enough that you should understand them, and talk to a tax professional (which I am not) about them, should you have the mixed blessing of hitting a four-digit exotic payoff.

The United States is one of the few countries that even taxes gambling winnings at all. While selfishly we might prefer this were not so, the idea that your net gambling winnings in the course of a full year should be tax-free is hard to defend. If that were as far as it went, most horseplayers probably would have no real objection to the idea of paying an income tax on their true year-end winnings. Unfortunately, the tax code goes far beyond that.

The IRS rules, formulated in the infancy of exotic betting, require that winnings at odds of 300-1 or higher be reported to the government if they exceed $600 and that the payoffs are subject to withholding if they total $5,000 or more. (That latter threshold was raised from $1,000 to $5,000 in the early 1990's, the last time the rules were changed.) Perhaps this was more palatable in the days when a daily double or exacta would pay off at 300-1 so rarely that such triumphs were true windfalls. Once trifectas and even more complex bets at those odds and payoffs became daily occurrences, however, the tax system became a nightmare for horseplayers.

There are several huge problems with this method of reporting and withholding:

1. *The IRS discriminates against horse racing and people who make exotic bets.*

   It makes no sense that a $7,350 collection on a win bet is not subject to reporting or withholding, but a $1,100 trifecta is. In addition, even bigger winners at casino games get off virtually scot-free. The casinos have successfully argued that when someone walks away from a dice table with $10,000 in chips, the house has no way of knowing whether he started out with $500 or $15,000. All that such a gambler has to do is cash out for less than $10,000 at a time—thereby avoiding another regulation regarding large cash transactions—and he can escape the requirements imposed on a small bettor who hits an occasional four-digit trifecta.

2. *The IRS reports and withholds based on gross winnings, not net profits.*

   No other business or activity is treated this way. Suppose that a store sells $1 million worth of mer-chandise in the course of a year, and its true profit after cost of goods, expenses, and payroll is $50,000. The business pays taxes on that $50,000 profit. If the IRS treated the store the way it treats horseplayers, it would confiscate $250,000 right off the top as 25 percent of the gross receipts. The store owner could apply for a refund, but would probably be out of business before receiving it up to a year later.

This is exactly what happens to an exotic bettor. If you lose $1,000 a day on Monday, Tuesday, Wednesday, and Thursday, then invest another $1,000 on Friday and hit a pick four for $5,100, you have bet $5,000 for the week and gotten a return of $5,100. Your profit is $100, and you probably wouldn't have a problem paying the government around $25 as income tax. Instead, the government seizes 25 percent of that $5,100 hit, which is $1,275, leaving you with $1,175 less cash than you had at the beginning of the week.

3. *The IRS explicitly says that every exotic payoff is the result of a single, independent $1 or $2 bet.*

Let's say you put $1,458 into a pick-six part-wheel using three horses in every race (not a recommended play, as we shall discuss later), a bunch of favorites win, and you hit it but the payoff is only $1,500. You won $42, hardly the 300-1 return that is supposed to trigger IRS involvement. The IRS, however, treats this "windfall" as if you bought a single $2 ticket on the winning combination and received a return of 749-1 on your money.

"For multiple wagers sold on one ticket," the IRS says in the 2006 version of its Instructions for Forms

W-2G and 5754, "such as the $12 box bet on a Big
Triple or Trifecta, the wager is considered as six $2
bets and not one $12 bet for purposes of computing
the amount to be reported or withheld. Winnings on a
$12 box bet must be reported if they are $600 or more,
and federal income tax must be withheld if the proceeds total more than $5,000."

This verbiage reflects how completely out of touch
the tax code is with modern betting, since the "$12
box bet" went the way of the dodo when tracks
dropped their minimum trifecta prices from $2 to $1
more than a decade ago, and "Big Triple" is a relic
from the 1970's.

The IRS's illogical insistence on treating multiple
bets this way is the source of the majority of withholding and reporting. If it only taxed the proceeds of
a $48 trifecta part-wheel when the return on total
investment was truly 300-1 or higher, it would require
a $14,448 return on a $48 bet for you to start filling out
forms.

4. *The IRS allows you to deduct losses against your
   winnings, but only as an itemized deduction, not as
   an adjustment to income.*

   You would think that if you bet $50,000 in the
   course of a year and got back $52,000, the IRS should
   be told that you made $2,000 and tax you accordingly,
   but you would be wrong. Instead, you are supposed
   to report $52,000 in income and then—and only if you
   itemize deductions—claim $50,000 in losses on a sep-
   arate part of your tax return as a deduction against the
   $52,000 in "winnings."

The problem here is that there can be adverse consequences to increasing your gross income, such as becoming subject to the Alternative Minimum Tax or reaching a threshold where other deductions are limited or phased out. Additionally, not everyone's circumstances make it possible or prudent to itemize deductions at all.

In fact, the letter of the IRS regulations compels you to do this even if you make nothing more than $2 win bets and even if you come out a loser for the year. Let's say you made 10 $2 win bets in the course of a day, catching two winners at $11.60 and $8.40 to break exactly even. Technically, you are supposed to increase your gross income by $20 and itemize $20 in losses against it.

There is probably not a single person in the United States who does this, and as a practical matter, this requirement is not observed or enforced by anyone. Yet exotic bettors are treated precisely this way simply because exotic betting is a game of peaks and valleys where infrequent triumphs make up for long stretches of losing bets.

For most players, the whole IRS issue amounts to an outrageous but manageable nuisance. The casual player who has a few "signers" and perhaps one instance of withholding for the year will, after receiving professional advice, probably deduct losses up to the amount of his reported so-called winnings, and should get back some or all of what was withheld—albeit after giving the government an interest-free loan for up to 18 months.

It becomes more burdensome the more you bet and win,

because the constant confiscation of 25 percent of your gross receipts on your best days will begin denting and perhaps consuming your bankroll. One of the nation's most successful exotics players says that his withholdings take away so much of his working capital by the final quarter of each year that he almost annually has to tap into a home-equity credit line just to have enough working capital until his massive annual tax refund arrives. He would be happy to pay quarterly estimated taxes on his actual winnings four times a year, even at the 25 percent rate, but the IRS refuses to treat even full-time professional gamblers this way.

What is almost as absurd as these regulations is the failure of the racing industry to get them revised. In 2003, the National Thoroughbred Racing Association took a step in the right direction, convening a Players' Panel of serious handicappers and bettors to make recommendations, and this issue was at the top of their list. However, industry officials have claimed they have been unable to make any progress on the matter, though they seem to be able to influence legislation with a more direct impact on powerful horse owners.

The supposed lack of headway on changing gambling withholdings seemed particularly disingenuous when, in 2004, racing lobbyists were successful in overturning a similar IRS regulation that previously had demanded a 30 percent withholding on all racetrack winnings by nonresidents betting into United States pools. This was an equally idiotic provision and based on a similar issue, but industry lobbyists were able to get it dropped as part of a "Jobs Creation Bill" passed by Congress. The change allowed U.S. tracks to increase their profits by accepting wagers from countries such as Canada, which previously had been forced to create their own smaller betting pools on U.S. racing. The industry's success with this bill, while failing to do anything about the W2-G situation for American bettors, made it appear that the industry either didn't understand or didn't care about the similar situation facing its own regular customers.

The shocking response of some track operators is that the withholding issue is not a big deal because bettors are so tickled to cash a signer that they barely even notice a tax deduction. If nothing else, this attitude is remarkably short-sighted in terms of the tracks' self-interest. Constant withholding removes money from the bettors' total available funds that would otherwise be repeatedly churned through the windows, increasing the industry's handle and profits.

Consider what happens in an exotic pool when the payoff is over $5,000. The Magna 5 is a five-leg multirace wager linking selected races at Gulfstream, Santa Anita, Laurel, and Golden Gate on winter and spring Saturdays. On January 28, 2006, the bet attracted a robust pool of over $600,000. There were 70 winners, producing an after-takeout return of $6,792.20 for each winning ticket. None of those ticket holders, however, received $6,792.20. Because the $2 payout exceeded $5,000 at odds of over 300-1, each was subject to 25 percent withholding, which worked out to $1,698 per ticket, reducing the $6,792.20 payout to $5,094.

Of the $470,000 or so due to be paid out to winning ticket holders, more than $115,000 was instead shipped straight to the Internal Revenue Service. According to some economic models, had that money not been taken out of circulation, it would have been churned at least five more times for an additional $500,000 in handle. Something similar happens every day with big pay-offs at tracks all across the country. Only recently have a few enlightened track operators begun to see that this adds up to tens if not hundreds of millions of dollars annually.

What is particularly unfortunate about the Magna 5—a bet that has frequently paid off in the $5,000 to $10,000 range—is that the entire withholding scenario could have been avoided if Magna offered the bet as a $1 rather than $2 minimum wager. At a payoff of $3,396.10 for $1 instead of $6,792.20 for $2, winners would still have had to report their winnings, but there would have been no withholding. Also, the bet would have been far more affordable for many players.

This brings us back, in a roundabout fashion, to the appeal of dime superfectas and the case for reducing minimum bets whenever possible. A superfecta that pays $48,000 for $1 will be reduced by $12,000 in federal withholding to a $36,000 payout. A dime superfecta that returns $4,800 for 10 cents will not be subject to withholding because it falls below the $5,000 threshhold. For that reason alone, superfecta players should strongly consider making their bets in dime increments wherever possible.

For the same reason, players should always buy their exotic tickets in $1 rather than $2 increments where available, even if that means buying the same ticket more than once. Don't be shy about it: There is a "repeat" button on most parimutuel machines and there's nothing untoward about buying a $1 part-wheel and then asking the clerk or operator to "repeat that ticket" one or more times. If you hit a trifecta that pays $650 for $2 on a $2 ticket, you will have to fill out a W-2G. Hit it for $325 twice on separate $1 tickets, and you can duck the paperwork.

What the IRS regulations have achieved above all is to create a thriving industry of illegal ticket-cashing. Many bettors, confused and frightened by the entire prospect of having any gambling activity reported to the government, seek out "ten-percenters," shady individuals with fake identification who loiter around every track in the country and will be glad to cash your ticket for an additional 10 percent of your ever-diminishing net. (Although they are still known as ten-percenters, the going rate at this writing has dropped to five percent for those who shop around.)

In addition to being illegal, patronizing ten-percenters is criminally stupid, depriving you of the opportunity to recover some or all of your withholdings at year's end, to which you will almost always be entitled. Remember, when the IRS withholds from a payout of $5,000 or more, they are making the assumption that you made a single winning $1 or $2 bet and are not giving you credit for all the other bets you made in order to get that payout, much less for your losing days. If you have legitimately come out on the negative end of the ledger at year's end, you should be able to get all of your withholdings back by taking a Schedule A itemized deduction of your losses against the full amount of your reported gross winnings.

Fortunately, the IRS seems to understand that horseplayers don't win every time they bet, or at least the agents I dealt with when I was twice audited for gambling deductions did. I arrived at the IRS offices with my detailed records of every bet I had made during the year, prepared to defend my deductions down to the penny, but the agents weren't interested in more than a cursory look at all my paperwork. In both cases, the six-figure deductions I had claimed against six-figure reported winnings had set off an automatic red flag and they really just wanted to confirm that I actually gambled regularly and wasn't somehow laundering money for criminals.

I didn't lose any sleep over those audits because I had complied with and probably exceeded the IRS's recommendations for record-keeping, as enumerated in IRS Publication 529, the 2006 version of which is excerpted below:

*You must report the full amount of your gambling win-
nings for the year on Form 1040, line 21. You deduct
your gambling losses for the year on Schedule A (Form
1040), line 27. You cannot deduct gambling losses that
are more than your winnings. You cannot reduce your
gambling winnings by your gambling losses and report
the difference. You must report the full amount of your
winnings as income and claim your losses (up to the
amount of winnings) as an itemized deduction.
Therefore, your records should show your winnings separately from your losses.*

Diary of winnings and losses. *You must keep an
accurate diary or similar record of your losses and
winnings.*

*Your diary should contain at least the following
information.*

1. *The date and type of your specific wager or
   wagering activity.*
2. *The name and address or location of the gambling
   establishment.*
3. *The names of other persons present with you at the
   gambling establishment.*
4. *The amount(s) you won or lost.*

Proof of winnings and losses. *In addition to your diary,
you should also have other documentation. You can generally prove your winnings and losses through Form W-2G,
Certain Gambling Winnings, Form 5754, Statement by
Person(s) Receiving Gambling Winnings, wagering tickets,
canceled checks, substitute checks, credit records, bank*

*withdrawals, and statements of actual winnings or pay-
ment slips provided to you by the gambling establishment.*

*For specific wagering transactions, you can use the fol-
lowing items to support your winnings and losses.*

*These recordkeeping suggestions are intended as gen-
eral guidelines to help you establish your winnings and
losses. They are not all-inclusive. Your tax liability
depends on your particular facts and circumstances. . . .*

***Racing (horse, harness, dog, etc.).** A record of the
races, amounts of wagers, amounts collected on winning
tickets, and amounts lost on losing tickets. Supplemental
records include unredeemed tickets and payment records
from the racetrack.*

This is not quite as burdensome as it may first appear, and
it gets you in the habit of keeping records of all your
wagering, which has numerous side benefits. Having a log of
all your wagers not only keeps you honest with yourself
about how you're doing but also allows you to analyze your
betting and see what you might actually be better or worse at
than you think.

When the pick four first came to New York, I jumped in
and played it with enthusiasm for a few months and felt I was
holding my own while getting accustomed to the wager. After
a while I broke down my recent betting by wager type and
discovered to my horror that I had frittered away over $10,000
on the bet and hadn't really noticed because of some offsetting successes in other pools. I belatedly realized I had been
playing the bet in what I now consider the "wrong" way, at
least for me—treating it like a pick three and trying to crush
a limited number of combinations instead of using a multiple-
ticket strategy with mains and backups at lower levels.

You can enter you results by hand into a notebook or, as I do, into a simple spreadsheet, which will then allow you to sort and analyze the data. I keep three separate logs: a master wager-by-wager record, a daily summary showing total wagering and net results for each track played each day, and a tax log listing all W-2G reporting and withholding transactions. This is five minutes' work at the end of each day and would be well worth the effort even if the IRS requirements did not exist.

Another IRS form you should know about is Form 5754, which can be used to carve up a tax ticket among more than one partner. When a group pools its money to play the pick six and hits it, there is often a panicky discussion of who should sign for the ticket and how to deal with tax liability and withholding. Instead, such a winning group can ask to cash the ticket together using Form 5754 and each partner will be given a separate W-2G reflecting only his percentage of the ticket.

Track and OTB mutuel departments will generally be helpful with navigating IRS problems. One unnecessary concern among some players who hit their first signer is that they may not be carrying a Social Security card and thus think they must resort to doing business with a ten-percenter. A polite phone call to the track mutuel department is a better idea, and alternate forms of identification are sometimes accepted. Still, if you're a regular exotic bettor who wagers in cash, it probably makes sense to carry a Social Security card.

Those betting outlets that offer account wagering can generate copies of your wagering history to prove offsetting losses, which provides a fallback for lazy players who do not keep their own betting logs. Dealing with tax tickets is itself a good reason for opening a wagering account. Once your account is established and your Social Security number has been verified, the signable and taxable tickets you buy through an account will be processed automatically and your W-2G's will be mailed to you.

Account wagering may ultimately offer the most realistic solution to the entire taxation mess. Most regular players who deal with multiple signers and withholdings in the course of a year would happily volunteer to have their account activity reported to the government at year's end in exchange for not having 25 percent of their best scores confiscated. If nothing else, the industry could work with the IRS to have the withholding rate for account-holders lowered from 25 to something like 10 percent to reflect the obvious fact that no one wins every day and that withholdings can often exceed a player's total profits for an entire year.

What would be even simpler and fairer would be to multiply the current reporting and withholding thresholds by a factor of 10, from $1,000 and $5,000 to $10,000 and $50,000. That way the government would still get its piece of true windfalls, ten-percenters would be driven out of business, and over 95 percent of current W-2G paperwork could be eliminated overnight.

Until that happens, players should be prepared for but not scared of the tax consequences of winning big exotic bets. In most cases, they will be able to deduct their legitimate losses against their winnings, eventually get back their withheld money, and perhaps in the process get into the good habit of keeping wagering records.

6 THE PICK SIX

THE PICK SIX holds a unique place in racetrack wagering that makes it an entirely different kind of bet from the other multirace exotics. Financially, it offers both spectacular payouts unavailable elsewhere and, through its unique carry-over provision, one of the few positive-expectation propositions in all of gambling. Emotionally, I consider it the ultimate handicapping challenge, a daunting and inspiring tournament among horseplaying's samurai warriors.

Yet realistically, I know it is a wager that most horseplayers should avoid except under very special and specific circumstances.

The origin of the pick six is widely credited to Caliente Race Track in Tijuana, Mexico, where it was offered as early as the 1930's under the names "49er" or "5-10," references to its encompassing Races 4 through 9 or 5 through 10 on the racecard. Bettors made out their selections manually on special slips, and track employees sat behind a huge glass window sorting through the slips after each race, marking which tickets were still "alive."

Marje Everett brought the bet to Hollywood Park when she owned it in the early 1980's, introducing automation by having the tote companies write new software to handle the bet and adding the carryover provision that would turn out to be the key to the popularity of the wager. The pick six quickly caught on nationally, coming to Florida in 1983 and New York in 1985, but has remained most popular in California.

Obviously, the pick six has two more legs than the already tricky and difficult pick four, making it that much harder to corral. With 10-horse fields, you're going from 10,000 possible outcomes in a pick four to 1,000,000 such pick-six possibilities. Even using the average eight-horse field, the number jumps from 4,096 to 262,144. Add in the fact that the pick six has a $2 rather than $1 minimum almost everywhere, something unlikely to change even if other bets become available at smaller increments, and it is a vastly more difficult proposition from its multirace brethren.

In the pick three and pick four, a lazy player with extra cash can make a loose part-wheel and "have it" fairly often. A 4 x 4 x 4 pick three costs $64 for $1, and a similar pick four runs $256. Suppose you're using the four favorites, one of whom wins any given race about 70 percent of the time. This makes you roughly 34 percent to hit such a 4 x 4 x 4 pick three (0.7 x 0.7 x 0.7) and 24 percent to hit that pick four. The problem is that they won't pay enough over the long run to get you close to even, although you'll cash plenty of tickets.

Applying such a strategy to the pick six, however, is simply unaffordable for 99 percent of players and would be ruinous for the 1 percent with that much money and that little sense. At a $2 minimum bet, taking the four favorites in each leg of the pick six will cost $8,192, and you're now only 12 percent to cash, meaning your *average* payoff would have to be nearly $70,000 just to break even.

Nowhere are the bankroll inequities among players more pronounced than in the pick six, simply because a modest investment buys so little coverage. Small players who put $16 or $24 or $48 into a pick six are buying very few combinations. I put in a minimum of $400 when I play the pick six, and even if someone putting in $32 is a better handicapper than I am, I just have far too great an advantage. I almost surely have all of his combinations covered, and many more.

Beyond the mathematical increases when you expand from three or four to six races, there is a threshold of competence that comes into play. When Seattle Slew was going for the Triple Crown in 1977, one detractor of jockey Jean Cruguet unkindly (and, as it turned out, inaccurately) wrote that the distance of the Belmont Stakes could be a problem because "a mile and a half is a long time for the Frenchman to go without making a mistake." In a similar vein, six races is a long time for a mediocre or slapdash handicapper to go without making a crucial miscalculation or omission. Put another way, it's a very long time to stay lucky.

Would the pick six be more accessible and affordable if the minimum were dropped from a deuce to a dime? Of course it would, but this is unlikely to happen and it is the one case where I don't think even I would argue that it should—solely because of the carryover factor.

Carryovers

Let's return for a moment to that party of 10 people gathered around a Florida dinner table, which we visited to illustrate how win-pool takeout works. As you'll remember, everyone put $20 into a kitty in the middle of the table and whoever picked the winner of the race took the pot—after the giant hand of takeout had extracted $30 of the $200.

This time, imagine that instead of picking a winner, each person tries to pick six consecutive winners in advance. Not surprisingly, none of the 10 does so. But now a couple of different things happen. First, because the takeout on the pick six is 25 percent in Florida, the giant hand helps itself to $50 rather than $30, leaving $150 in the kitty. If two people had picked six, each would have gotten $75. But since no one picked six, here's what happens instead. First, 25 percent of that $150, or $37.50, is paid out to those who picked the most winners. Let's say two people did; they would each get a "consolation" payoff of $18.75 (or $18.60 after breakage).

That leaves $112.50 in the pot. The good news is that neither the host nor the giant hand gets to keep this money just because no one went 6 for 6 today. Instead, the $112.50 is put into the cutlery drawer overnight for safekeeping, and everyone is invited back to the table tomorrow for a new sequence of six races. When they show up the next day and put their $20 bills in the middle, the giant hand reaches in and grabs another $50 in takeout. But then the $112.50 comes out of the cutlery drawer and is added to the remaining $150 from the Day 2 pot, for a total of $262.50.

Think for a moment about what this means. Today, if someone picks six, the payout pool is $262.50 even though only $200 was wagered into today's pot. Instead of the giant hand reducing today's pool by $50, the more benevolent hand of the carryover has increased today's pool from $200 to $262.50—sort of a 31.25 percent put-back, instead of a 25 percent takeout.

You didn't have to play on Day 1 in order to play on Day 2—in fact, the table is likely to be more crowded than it was the day before because of people like me, who rarely play the pick six unless there is a carryover and then come to the party when there's free money in the middle of the table. Simply put, I obviously would rather play when there is $62.50 more than there should be in the kitty than when there is $50 less.

Let's look at how this might work with our kitchen-table example if nobody picks six for a couple of days and the pool grows 100 percent each day as interest mounts in the carryover:

Day	Bet	-Takeout	+Carry	Net Pool	Consos	New Carry
1	$ 200	-$ 50	—	$ 150.00	-$ 37.50	$ 112.50
2	$ 400	-$100	+112.50	$ 412.50	-$ 75.00	$ 337.50
3	$ 800	-$200	+337.50	$ 937.50	-$150.00	$ 787.50
4	$1,600	-$400	+787.50	$1,987.50	-$300.00	$ 1,687.50

Note that the carryover is not subjected to repeated takeouts; after the first time it is taxed, it carries over in its entirety until it is distributed. Note also that even though the handle is growing each day, the pool becomes even more favorable as the carryover builds. On Day 2, the payout pool of $412.50 is only 3 percent higher than the $400 bet that day. By Day 4, though, the payout pool of $1,987.50 is nearly 25 percent higher than the $1,600 wagered into the pool that day.

Carryovers will continue this way until someone eventually picks six. At smaller tracks with tiny pools that are not going to inspire new and more serious investments until there are numerous carryovers, this can go on for a week or more. In California and New York, there is a one-day carryover once or twice a week and a two-day carryover about every other week. They build quickly and geometrically. A few times a year, there is a three-day carryover, which ensures a pool of over $1 million, setting up the possibility of life-changing payouts.

As for dropping the pick-six minimum, tracks are understandably uninterested because there would be far fewer carryovers if players could buy 20 times as many combinations for the same investment. The extra money bet when there is a carryover has become a significant part of tracks' revenue streams, especially in California, where track officials talk about the number of carryovers in their meeting-end financial statements.

The growth of simulcasting has had a huge influence on the popularity of the pick six. As the bet first became available in the 1980's, it was limited to its live local audience, but this began to change as most jurisdictions allowed full-card simulcasting in the 1990's. Now someone sitting in Chicago could wait for a carryover to occur in New York or California and jump into the pool the next day, only playing when there was both a jackpot and a favorable situation due to "free" carryover money.

That led to the growth of "syndicate" betting, where organized groups were formed solely to make large investments in carryovers, using the leverage of a big bankroll in an attempt to scoop the pool. This has caused some smaller players to think that they should avoid carryovers and perhaps instead play only on non-carryover days, when they won't be so outgunned by large investors, but this puts them in the position of not playing on precisely those days when payoffs will be larger than they should be.

The beauty of carryovers is that they work for both large players and the smaller ones who probably should be playing *only* under these circumstances—and not because they have a realistic chance at a seven-digit payout. Why small players may want to consider jumping into big carryovers is not because their $24 is going to include a combination that someone playing for $1,000 or $10,000 has overlooked, but because the payoff for the occasional sextet of obvious, logical favorites is going to pay so extraordinarily well. A string of six short prices that might yield a crummy $800 payoff on a non-carryover day might pay $4,000 or $5,000, not only because of the free money that has been added to the pool, but also because the heavy investors have actually underbet these combinations by shooting for the moon.

Big players are not going to buy the combination of the six logical favorites an extra 5 or 10 times. That money is better spent adding a single longshot somewhere on one of their tickets who might, even if it's only once a decade or a lifetime, trigger a six-figure return.

What players who can afford only a modest pick-six investment should consider is not only waiting for carryovers but also forming their own mini-syndicates, pooling their money with a few friends to get better leverage. A $128 ticket split four ways buys a far greater chance of success than four individual $32 plays. An extreme extension of this idea is the recent offering by one account-wagering company of a "Players' Pool," where small investors can buy tiny fractional pieces of a very large ticket.

The other thing that all pick-six players should do is consider multiple-ticket rather than single-ticket investments. Even at a low level of play, an array of main and backup horses is going to give you more flexibility than a one-ticket punch where you will be under- and overemphasizing individual horses without affording yourself a chance to be at least slightly "wrong" in one or even two races, while still eligible to collect if you are very "right" in the four or five others.

Pick-Six Tickets

I learned the basics of multiple-ticket pick-sixing as a minority member of a press-box syndicate Andrew Beyer had invited me to join in Florida in the winter of 1984. Beyer had come up with the idea of buying one or two "backup" tickets to go along with his primary one-ticket play. Suppose the group was putting $720 into a carryover. A single-ticket play would have eaten up that investment with one ticket such as this:

Race A: 1,3,5
Race B: 7
Race C: 2,4
Race D: 3,6,9,10,12
Race E: 5,8
Race F: 4,6,7,8,9,11
(3 x 1 x 2 x 5 x 2 x 6 = 360 combinations @ $2 = $720)

The problem races were not the ones where the group was willing to live or die with only one or two horses. Those were the strongest opinions of the day, and that's why they call it gambling. What we wanted was even more coverage in the toughest races on the card—say, two more horses in Race D and four more in Race F—but simply adding those six horses to the ticket would have jumped the cost from $720 to $1,680.

Instead, we would winnow those two tough races even further and classify a small number of the horses as mains and the rest as backups. Here's how it worked:

	Mains	**Backups**
Race A:	1,3,5	
Race B:	7	
Race C:	2,4	
Race D:	3,6	8,9,10,11,12
Race E:	5,8	
Race F:	4,6	1,2,3,5,7,8,9,11

Instead of putting in a single ticket, you would now put in three different tickets as follows:

	Ticket 1 (Mains Only)	**Ticket 2** (Backup D)	**Ticket 3** (Backup F)
Race A:	1,3,5	1,3,5	1,3,5
Race B:	7	7	7
Race C:	2,4	2,4	2,4
Race D:	3,6	8,9,10,11,12	3,6
Race E:	5,8	5,8	5,8
Race F:	4,6	4,6	1,2,3,5,7,8,9,11
Ticket Cost:	$96	$240	$384

For the same $720, we now had options in Races D and F if we had thinned down the mains correctly. (As a practical matter, Tickets 1 and 2 could be combined into a single $336 ticket reading 1,3,5/7/2,4/3,6,8,9,10,11,12/5,8/4,6.)

When I began playing the pick six on my own when it came to New York a year later, I took this idea a step or two further, expanding from mains and backups to A's, B's, and C's and making out as many as 30 tickets covering various permutations among them.

Over the years, friends with programming skills have offered to write simple software that would automate the laborious process of writing out those combinations by hand, and there are several commercial programs on the market that can accomplish this. Personally, though, I prefer to do it all by hand in a bound graph-paper notebook because I find myself constantly tinkering with and adjusting tickets, and because I'm a creature of habit.

Then and now, I don't even think about structuring a pick-six investment until I'm done with my analysis of the races. It's impossible not to have some passing thoughts along the lines of "I may end up singling this horse" or "This looks like a messy race where I'm going to want a lot of coverage." The first time through a card, though, I have found it is better just to concentrate on the horses and races without jumping to conclusions about how you will bet.

When I am ready to start crafting a play, I begin by making out exactly the kind of ticket I don't recommend as an entire play—a ticket of just my A horses, which if possible includes two potential singles. I have found that an ideal starting point is a main ticket like this that includes roughly two singles, two doubles, and two triples. If this comprised an entire invest-ment, it would be a $72 ticket:

1,2
1
1,2,3
1,2
1,2,3
1

(2 x 1 x 3 x 2 x 3 x 1 = 36 combos @ $2 = $72)

Again, I would never simply stop here and invest $72 in a pick six. I just don't think it's enough coverage to have a real-istic chance, and I don't expect to be this precisely "right" six times in a row. Try making out some 1 x 1 x 2 x 2 x 3 x 3 plays like this and you will find that you'll often go 4 for 6 or 5 for 6 but rarely 6 for 6—and that, in a way, is exactly what I'm hoping for. Those rare occasions when you do get six A's to win are probably the days when nothing interesting hap-pens and the pick six pays less than $1,000. If, however, I can get home four or five of my A's and use the right B's and/or C's on backup tickets, I could be looking at a healthy payoff.

There are days when the first pass through a card won't get you anywhere close to a manageable play, much less a mere $72 ticket of A's. At that point, the first thing to do is question whether your handicapping was sloppy and you need to go through the card again. If not, it may be a day to take a pass. Much as it pains me to pass up a carryover in New York, there are days when I just don't have a handle on several of the races in the sequence, can't see a potential single anywhere, and will reluctantly sit it out and root for another carryover.

If I do think it's playable, my next step is to add my B's and C's to the array and start figuring out the number and cost of the various backup tickets. You can't have multiple B's and C's in every race without your play quickly becoming astro-nomical. My own personal-comfort range is between $500 and $2,500, depending on the size of the carryover and my enthusiasm for the proposition. It's useful to have such limits in mind, or you will end up carefully classifying every pos-sible winner on a card and see that it would cost you some-thing like $10,000 to jump in.

Probably the biggest mistake that ambitious pick-six players make is to think they have to be contrary and smart-alecky throughout the card. When playing individual races, or even a short multirace sequence, it may well make sense to play against favorites you acknowledge can win but might be vulnerable, but taking this approach in the pick six is going to leave you tearing up tickets. If there's some 15-1 shot on the card you think should be half that price, there are many other and better ways to play him instead of singling him in the pick six. You might well want to make such a horse an A because of the combination of likelihood and value, but it would be better to make him one of two or three A's than to stand alone with a horse you would admit is no better than 12 or 15 percent to win the race.

There is absolutely nothing wrong with singling an odds-on favorite as part of the pick six just because he's going to be "everyone's" single. The tough races are tough enough without pretending that the easy races are more complicated than they are. Your goal is to get through all six races, not to make six different interesting things happen—it only takes one or two such things to make a pick six very worthwhile.

The following two examples are actual pick-six plays that I made while writing this book during the second half of 2005. I have chosen them not because of their somewhat happy endings or to suggest regular success—there are plenty of days when I miss by a mile. Rather, they illustrate the very different ways that the sequence can unfold while touching on several issues associated with playing the bet.

Saratoga Sixes

Saratoga is my favorite place to play the pick six, for a variety of reasons. It is summer camp for New York horseplayers, where you immerse yourself in handicapping and horses all day long without distraction from the so-called real world. On a more venal note, the pools are looser than at any time of the year in New York, swelled with uninformed money from tourists and other casual players. I try to play every carryover during the meeting and will play the weekend pick sixes even without a carryover because there's effectively free money in the pool anyway due to the tourist trade.

The Friday, August 12, card had a one-day carryover of $64,768 and not a lot else to recommend it except a couple of potential singles late in the day. Here was what my post-handicapping array looked like:

Race	A Horses	B Horses	C Horses	X Horses
4th	2,5	3,4	6,7	1,8,9
5th	2,4,5	—	—	1,3,6
6th	1,8,9	—	3,5,6,7	2,4
7th	3,8	7,12	—	1,2,4,5,6,9,10,11
8th	8	4	—	1,2,3,7,9
9th	11	2	—	1,3,4,5,6,7,8,9,10

A single caveman ticket combining all my non-X horses would have required a 6 x 3 x 7 x 4 x 2 x 2 part-wheel for $4,032, a lot more than the maximum of $1,000 I wanted to spend. By taking the multiple-ticket route, I was able to keep my cost to $960 by making an array of tickets where I could win with either six A's; five A's and one B; five A's and one C; or four A's and two B's. This required making out 12 tickets, as follows:

Ticket 1	Ticket 2	Ticket 3	Ticket 4	Ticket 5	Ticket 6
2,5	**3,4,6,7**	2,5	2,5	2,5	2,5
2,4,5	2,4,5	2,4,5	2,4,5	2,4,5	2,4,5
1,8,9	1,8,9	**3,5,6,7**	1,8,9	1,8,9	1,8,9
3,8	3,8	3,8	**7,12**	3,8	3,8
8	8	8	8	**4**	8
11	11	11	11	11	**2**
$72	$144	$96	$72	$72	$72

Ticket 7	Ticket 8	Ticket 9	Ticket 10	Ticket 11	Ticket 12
3,4	**3,4**	**3,4**	2,5	2,5	2,5
2,4,5	2,4,5	2,4,5	2,4,5	2,4,5	2,4,5
1,8,9	1,8,9	1,8,9	1,8,9	1,8,9	1,8,9
7,12	3,8	3,8	**7,12**	**7,12**	3,8
8	**4**	8	**4**	8	**4**
11	11	**2**	11	**2**	**2**
$72	$72	$72	$72	$72	$72

Let's be clear on what these various tickets accomplish relative to the A-B-C breakdown above.

Ticket 1 is the starting-point all-A main ticket.

Tickets 2 through 6 are the five tickets that contain five A's plus one B or C. The race in which B's or C's are swapped in for a main are in boldface type. Note that there is no ticket with B's or C's for the second race in the sequence because in that race I had three A's and no backups.

Tickets 7 through 12 are the six permutations of four A's and two B's, with the two B's boldfaced on each ticket. For example, Ticket 7 uses the B horses in the first and fourth legs with A's in the others; Ticket 8 uses the B's in the first and fifth legs, etc.

The first unusual thing about this particular day was that my two singles came in the last two legs. If you had your choice, you would prefer that your singles came sooner in the card, not only to end the suspense early but also because you can't really do a lot of hedging if you get to the last two races and are alive just 1 x 1 to the two favorites.

Unfortunately, I didn't have the luxury of rearranging the races, and actually I had to be thankful that the track had thoughtfully put the first leg where they did, because it was a nine-horse field of maiden 2-year-old fillies that included four first-time starters. The firsters were particularly crucial because, of the five who had already run, only two seemed even vaguely related to Thoroughbreds. The other three had shown no ability and done so repeatedly.

I didn't finalize my A-B-C breakdown of my top six fillies— the two who had run decently and the four firsters—until I saw the early betting on the race, an opportunity that was available because of its position as the opening leg of the pick six. (Not all tracks are this accommodating. In California, for example, a firster-laden maiden race is often carded as the last race of the day, which management thinks is more fun because it leads to higher payouts. I would argue that it rewards insider knowledge, deprives bettors of crucial information, and makes playing the pick six less inviting.)

With 10 minutes to post, the four firsters were 2-1, 9-1, 11-1, and 15-1. I made the horse who had run best and the 2-1 firster my two A's; the 9-1 and 11-1 firsters my two B's; and the remaining firster and the most lightly raced and least horrible of the others with experience my two C's.

The 9-1 firster, who drifted to 11-1 by post time, was a 1 1/2-length winner over the 2-1 firster, who had dipped to 8-5 by post time, with my other A running third. The good news was that I had started the sequence with a $25.80 winner. The bad news was that I had already used up one of my B opportunities. Eight of my 12 tickets were dead after just one leg, and I now needed either five A's, or four A's and one B, the rest of the way. But at least I was alive, which I would not have been had I tried to shave down that $4,032 one-ticket play to under $1,000 by whittling away marginal horses, since I might well have begun by going only two-deep in the opening leg and quite possibly eliminating the winner.

My four remaining live tickets (numbers 2, 7, 8, and 9, for those keeping score) survived the next leg when one of my three A's in a six-horse field won at $7.80. I now faced a decision about whether to play the pick four on the last four races of the day as a saver to my pick-six position. I decided that the one thing that would drive me crazy would be if two B's won in the remaining four races, which would mean I had brilliantly zigzagged my way out of the pick six by the way I had split my A's and B's. So I bought what I like to call insanity insurance by buying precisely those "two B's" combinations—in effect, the last four legs of pick-six tickets 10, 11, and 12. In $1 increments, these tickets cost only $6 each, for a total of $18, so I bought them for $5 each, increasing my outlay for the whole endeavor from $960 (my pick-six investment) to $1,050 ($960 plus $90 worth of pick fours).

The next two races broke perfectly for me, as I got the best-priced A's home at $18 and $16.80. I can't claim I preferred these horses to my other A's, and these are the kinds of results where you consider yourself lucky to have survived (the second-place finishers in both races were X horses) and very lucky that things broke the best way for you.

With winners at $25.80, $7.80, $18, and $16.80 to my credit, I could now only hope to get through the last two races, the ones where I thought there was a horse who towered over the field in each leg. Even if the two favorites won, the payoff had to be decent. In addition, I had the opportunity to beat one or the other with my one B in each race, because after a 3-4-9-8 start, I still had three live tickets:

Ticket 2	Ticket 8	Ticket 9
3,4,6,7	3,4	3,4
2,4,5	2,4,5	2,4,5
1,8,9	1,8,9	1,8,9
3,8	3,8	3,8
8	4	8
11	11	2

If the 8 horse won the fifth leg, I would be alive to both the 2 and the 11 in the finale, and if the 4 won the race, I would be alive only to the 11. The nightmare of a B-B conclusion to the sequence if it ended 4-2 was somewhat mitigated by that $5 pick-four ticket that couldn't be too bad itself.

All I could do was sit back and watch things unfold in the penultimate race of the day, the Waya Stakes for turf mares at a mile and a half. Grass marathons are one of my least favorite and least successful handicapping propositions, but even I had been able to figure out that there was a mismatch here: Latice, who had won the Grade 1 French Oaks a year earlier, was meeting a ragtag group of allowance horses and would jog if trainer Jonathan Sheppard had her even 90 percent ready off an eight-month layoff. He did, Latice paid $4, and I was now alive to both my A and B in the last race.

When the pick-six probables were posted, I saw there would be a rather significant difference. If my A, Elisa's Energy, won as the 3-5 favorite, I would be one of nine winners at $31,407. If my B, Alley Singer, were to score the mild upset as the 7-2 second choice, I would be one of only three winners at $94,221 apiece. After silently cursing the two other Saratoga pick-six players on the planet who had cut my possible return with Alley Singer from a pool-scooping $282,663 to a mere $94,221, I turned my attention to the possibility of hedging.

Since I was alive to only two horses in a field of 12, it was going to be difficult to bet savers and truly hedge my position. My 10 uncovered horses ranged from 8-1 to 87-1, but betting them all to win was only going to get me about a 3-2 blended return. (I know it feels like it should be more, but I later did the math and it would have required a total of $2,006 in win bets to get a return of exactly $5,000 on each of the 10 other horses in the race.)

Was it worth it to bet $2,000 to get $5,000, or $4,000 to get $10,000, as a hedge against my getting $31,407 or $94,221 if one of my two live horses won? As a straightforward proposition in isolation, the answer was clearly no. I truly thought Elisa's Energy—who had been running Beyer Speed Figures in the high 70's against open maiden company in California and now was facing restricted New York-breds who rarely cracked 65 on their best days—just about had to fall down to lose. If she did, Alley Singer, who had run a troubled 68 in her grass debut, would beat the others with just a repeat of that effort. Between them I felt like I was about 90 percent to win, so I needed 9-1 and not a paltry 3-2 to make it a good bet.

Still, the situation is different when you're *guaranteed* $31,407 or $94,221 the 90 percent of the time you're right and looking at $0 the 10 percent of the time you're wrong. Then, fortunately, before spending $2,000 or $4,000, I realized I wasn't exactly looking at $0 if both of my horses somehow lost.

Whether or not the pick six is hit on any given day, 25 percent of that day's post-takeout pool is paid out to those tickets that have five of the six winners. (On those rare occasions when no one comes up with even five, the same amount is split up among those tickets with four winners.) People who don't play the pick six assume that the 5-of-6 payout goes only to those bettors who fail to hit the big prize, but in fact most of the consolation payouts go to those who have the major award as well. Suppose you (ill-advisedly) buy a pick-six ticket that reads 1/1/1/1/1/1,2,3,4 for $8. If number 1 wins every race, you have the 1-1-1-1-1-1 pick six, but you also have three 5-of-6 combinations on that same ticket—the 1-1-1-1-1-2, 1-1-1-1-1-3, and 1-1-1-1-1-4. Every "miss," or losing horse, on a winning pick-six ticket creates a consolation ticket as well.

I wasn't concerned about the consos I'd be getting in addition to the $31,407 or $94,221 if one of my horses won, but it belatedly occurred to me that I'd be looking at pretty decent payoffs for two 5-of-6 tickets (the 3-4-9-8-8-2 and the 3-4-9-8-8-11) if they both lost. An additional $387,368 had been bet on top of the $64,768 carryover, so $72,631 was going to be paid out in consos whether or not the pick six was hit. In addition to the nine live tickets to Elisa's Energy and the three to Alley Singer, there were only six other tickets alive. If some crazy 40-1 shot won, those 18 live tickets, and perhaps just a few nuts who had used the 40-1 shot but omitted an earlier winner, would be splitting up $72,631, so even if I missed I was looking at a few thousand in consos.

I didn't need to be betting $2,000 or $4,000 at 3-2. I settled for betting $500 to win on the lone first-time starter in the race, who was taking a little bit of action at 11-1, just in case she was a killer in disguise. If one of the known quantities beat me, I would console myself with the consolations.

The first-time starter beat one horse and Alley Singer didn't give me a moment of excitement running a dull fourth, but

Elisa's Energy never provided an anxious moment, cruising to an easy victory to secure the $31,407 payoff. The $90 pick-four saver and the $500 win bet on the dreadful firster were more than offset by the 14 consolations at $233.50 apiece. That meant that 14 other horses on the card could have won and I still would have had the pick six. A few of those 14, like Alley Singer, would have increased the payoff, while more of them would have knocked down the price. Like most things in life, it could have been better, but could have been worse.

There was only one sure thing: Despite my having invested $1,550 for the day, and despite my having been stuck $7,000 for Saratoga until Elisa's Energy was declared the official winner, my partner the Internal Revenue Service was there to extract its 25 percent of my supposed $31,407-for-$2 windfall, taking $7,851 right off the top. It should have been $7,851.75, but Uncle Sam benevolently lets you keep the change.

NINTH RACE
Saratoga
AUGUST 12, 2005

1⅛ MILES. (Turf) (1.45²) MAIDEN SPECIAL WEIGHT . Purse $46,000 FOR MAIDENS, FILLIES AND MARES THREE YEARS OLD AND UPWARD FOALED IN NEW YORK STATE AND APPROVED BY THE NEW YORK STATE-BRED REGISTRY. Three Year Olds, 118 lbs.; Older, 123 lbs. (Non-starters For A Claiming Price Less Than $35,000 In The Last 3 Starts Preferred). (If the Stewards consider it inadvisable to run this race on the turf course, this race will be run at One Mile and One Eighth on the main track.). (Rail at 12 feet).

Value of Race: $46,000 Winner $27,600; second $9,200; third $4,600; fourth $2,300; fifth $1,380; sixth $132; seventh $132; eighth $132; ninth $132; tenth $132; eleventh $132; twelfth $128. Mutuel Pool $599,751.00 Exacta Pool $562,106.00 Trifecta Pool $494,519.00 Superfecta Pool $253,485.00

Last Raced	Horse	M/Eqt.	A.	Wt	PP	St	¼	½	¾	Str	Fin	Jockey	Odds $1
9Jly05 ^{6}Hol^{3}	Elisa's Energy	L	3	118	11	10	4^{1}	$3^{1\frac{1}{2}}$	3^{1}	$1^{2\frac{1}{2}}$	$1^{2\frac{1}{4}}$	Prado E S	0.75
21Jly05 ^{2}Bel^{5}	ContendersEmotion	L	4	123	6	6	5^{hd}	4^{hd}	4^{hd}	$3^{2\frac{1}{2}}$	$2^{1\frac{3}{4}}$	Sutherland C	31.75
21Jly05 ^{2}Bel^{2}	Fiddlers Pleasure	L b	3	118	4	3	$6^{2\frac{1}{2}}$	7^{hd}	7^{2}	2^{hd}	$3^{3\frac{3}{4}}$	Migliore R	8.30
21Jly05 ^{9}Bel^{2}	Alley Singer	L	3	118	2	1	$7^{\frac{1}{2}}$	6^{hd}	$8^{4\frac{1}{2}}$	5^{5}	$4^{1\frac{1}{4}}$	Velasquez C	3.80
5Aug05 ^{1}Sar^{7}	Sogno Dolce	L	3	118	10	8	$2^{1\frac{1}{2}}$	$2^{\frac{1}{2}}$	2^{hd}	$4^{\frac{1}{2}}$	$5^{2\frac{3}{4}}$	Fragoso P	87.75
24Jun05 ^{6}Bel^{3}	Innis North	L	3	118	12	11	10^{hd}	11^{1}	11^{6}	6^{hd}	$6^{2\frac{1}{2}}$	Jara F	31.75
21Jly05 ^{2}Bel^{6}	Lear's Ruby	b	3	118	5	7	3^{hd}	$5^{1\frac{1}{2}}$	$5^{\frac{1}{2}}$	7^{hd}	$7^{2\frac{3}{4}}$	Espinoza J L	71.75
13Jly05 ^{9}Bel^{6}	Belahan	L	4	123	8	12	$11^{\frac{1}{2}}$	$8^{1\frac{1}{2}}$	$6^{\frac{1}{2}}$	9^{12}	8^{3}	Coa E M	39.00
20Jly05 ^{1}Bel^{4}	Conquest Bound	L	3	118	7	4	$1^{1\frac{1}{2}}$	1^{hd}	1^{hd}	8^{2}	$9^{11\frac{1}{4}}$	Castellano J J	14.00
21Jly05 ^{9}Bel^{6}	Tap the Magic	L bf	4	123	9	9	12	$10^{1\frac{1}{2}}$	$9^{\frac{1}{2}}$	10^{2}	10no	Lakeman A	41.50
	Behrenessa	L b	3	118	1	2	9^{hd}	9^{hd}	$10^{\frac{1}{2}}$	11^{15}	$11^{27\frac{3}{4}}$	Velazquez J R	11.90
15Jly05 ^{9}Bel^{9}	Breathalyzer	L b	3	118	3	5	$8^{1\frac{1}{2}}$	12	12	12	12	Rodriguez R R	69.50

OFF AT 5:22 Start Good. Won driving. Course firm.

TIME :23², :48⁴, 1:13⁴, 1:38³, 1:51¹ (:23.47, :48.90, 1:13.83, 1:38.77, 1:51.25)

$2 Mutuel Prices:

11 – ELISA'S ENERGY	3.50	2.70	2.20
6 – CONTENDERS EMOTION		12.00	5.30
4 – FIDDLERS PLEASURE			3.30

$2 EXACTA 11–6 PAID $97.50 $2 TRIFECTA 11–6–4 PAID $448.00
$2 SUPERFECTA 11–6–4–2 PAID $1,089.00

Dk. b or br. f, (Mar), by Chester House – Merion Miss, by Halo. Trainer Frankel Robert. Bred by Berkshire Stud and Oak Cliff Stable (NY).

ELISA'S ENERGY raced close up outside while in hand, rallied three wide on the second turn and drew clear when roused. CONTENDERS EMOTION raced close up outside, rallied into the stretch and finished gamely to earn the place award. FIDDLERS PLEASURE was rated along inside, rallied four wide approaching the stretch and finished well outside. ALLEY SINGER raced wide and had no response when roused. SOGNO DOLCE was hustled outside, contested the pace while between rivals and tired in the stretch. INNIS NORTH was outrun early, raced four wide and had no rally. LEAR'S RUBY chased the pace along the inside and tired in the stretch. BELAHAN was pinched back at the start, ducked in after start, was bumped, was taken up, raced wide and tired. CONQUEST BOUND was bumped at the start, was hustled to the front, set the pace along the inside and tired in the stretch. TAP THE MAGIC was bumped at the start and was outrun. BEHRENESSA was bumped after the start, was taken up, raced greenly and tired. BREATHALYZER tired badly and was eased in the stretch.

Owners– 1, Oak Cliff Stable and Galatyn Stables; 2, Flying Zee Stable; 3, Fiddlers Green Stable; 4, Casby Camelia J; 5, Walsh Elizabeth; 6, Coffeepot Stables; 7, Twin Pines Farm; 8, Curley John; 9, Oliva Stable; 10, Barely Stable and Summit View Farm; 11, Bond Tina M; 12, Bill O'Toole Stables

Trainers– 1, Frankel Robert; 2, Martin Frank; 3, Contessa Gary C; 4, Hennig Mark; 5, Cedano Heriberto; 6, Turner William H Jr; 7, Sciacca Gary; 8, Violette Richard A Jr; 9, Hertler John O; 10, Disanto Glenn B; 11, Bond Harold James; 12, Correa Jeff

Scratched– Lucky Genia (21Jul05 ^{9}Bel^{9}), Love My Gal (31Jul05 ^{2}Sar^{3}), My Niece Cayla (24Jul05 ^{5}Bel^{2})

$2 Daily Double (8–11) Paid $6.00 ; Daily Double Pool $360,369 .
$2 Pick Three (8–8–11) Paid $53.50 ; Pick Three Pool $203,568 .
$2 Pick Four (9–8–8–11) Paid $485.00 ; Pick Four Pool $330,336 .
$2 Pick Six (4–4–9–8–8–11) 6 Correct Paid $31,407.00 ; Pick Six Pool $387,368 .
$2 Pick Six (4–4–9–8–8–11) 5 Correct Paid $233.50 .

Saratoga Attendance: 23,504 Mutuel Pool: $3,570,708.00 ITW Mutuel Pool: $3,442,044.00 ISW Mutuel Pool: $6,131,552.00

A Rainy Day

New York Showcase Day, an afternoon of stakes races for New York-breds each October, is not typical of the nationally important graded-stakes racing you get on most fall weekends at Belmont Park, but it is actually one of the best betting cards of the year. The fields are usually full and the races frequently come up in a fashion that appeals to my style of multirace betting: There are often one or two mismatches where one legitimately good statebred is facing vastly overmatched local competition, and a few nearly impossible fields of horses who have taken turns beating one another for most of the year.

I was looking forward to the 2005 rendition, held at Belmont on October 22, one week before the Breeders' Cup, until the morning of the races. It was pouring, the track was a mess of slop, and an hour before post time, management reluctantly took all the afternoon's grass races off the turf, even a pair of six-figure Showcase races. The two grass stakes had been the most interesting of all the Showcase events and now figured to be uncompetitive races among the few remaining starters with any main-track ability.

My first impulse was to skip betting on the rainy festivities altogether and get a head start on my Breeders' Cup handicapping, but I went ahead and made my usual array, thinking I would probably limit myself to a pick-four play on the last four Showcase races. It looked like this:

Race	A Horses	B Horses	C Horses	X Horses
5th	12	—	—	1,2,3,4,5,6,7,8,9,10,11
6th	1	3,11	—	2,4,5,6,7,8,9,10,12
7th	1,11	—	9,12,14	3,6,7,8
8th	7,8	2,6	—	1,3,4,5
9th	3,7	6,9,10	—	1,2,4,5,8,11,12,13
10th	3,4	7,10	1,11	2,5,6,12

Only when I saw the way this shaped up did I even consider playing the pick six. There was no carryover from the previous day, and the horrendous weather was likely to keep the usually robust Saturday handle down. I of course wasn't going to put in the $3,600 that a single ticket with all my live horses would have required, and I wasn't sure I even wanted to spend the $640 that a typical A-B-C play would have required. But as long as I was thinking of playing the pick four, why not try to turn the pick six into a pick four by starting out with just my two singles on over 80 percent of my play? I decided to turn all my second-leg B's into C's and to allow myself three B's in the final three races. If I could get alive with a 1 x 1 x 2 to start out, why not have the luxury of a 4 x 5 x 4 spread in the last three?

Ticket 1	Ticket 2	Ticket 3	Ticket 4
12	12	12	12
1	3,11	1	1
1,11	1,11	9,12,14	1,11
2,6,7,8	7,8	7,8	7, 8
3,6,7,9,10	3,7	3,7	3,7
3,4,7,10	3,4	3,4	1,11
$320	$64	$48	$32

After putting in the tickets, I realized that from the total of $464, exactly $400 (Tickets 1, 3, and 4) was on tickets that began only 12-1. I wasn't crazy about having essentially made a $400 cold-punch double or parlay on two favorites on a sloppy track. Still, I rationalized, it would keep me out of trouble on the first two races where I otherwise had no good "underneath" ideas, and maybe something interesting would happen later on.

Both singles won, with Cinderella's Dream (number 12) paying $3.40 and Seeking the Ante (number 1) returning $6.30. A $400 parlay of the two of them would have come back $2,142, and I still had to get through four more races. If nothing but favorites won the rest of the way, I probably wouldn't even do that well.

The next three races all went to A's, at mutuels of $13.80, $8.60, and $5.30, hardly the prices I was hoping for with a 2 x 4 x 5 x 4 spread on my big ticket, and I resigned myself to having had a fairly unproductive day even if I hit the pick six. As the probable payoffs came up, I saw that two of them were worse than the win parlay of my two singles would have been and the other two were only about two and three times as good:

3	West Virginia	$ 1,560
4	Yankee Mon	$ 1,796
7	Naughty New Yorker	$ 4,235
10	Galloping Grocer	$ 6,588

It took me another minute to realize I had two additional possibilities. By getting home five A's, Ticket 4, the smallest of the batch at a mere $32, was still alive to my fifth and sixth choices in the finale, the wide-open $250,000 Empire Classic:

1	Spite the Devil	$19,765
11	Carminooch	$11,859

These probables illustrate the inordinate value of getting past the two, three, or four favorites in a pick-six race. There was $59,295 to be paid out for 6 of 6, so it's not difficult to see how many tickets were alive to each horse in the Classic:

Horse		P6 Payoff	Live Tickets
1	Spite the Devil	$19,765	3
2	Runingforpresident	$59,295	1
3	West Virginia	$ 1,560	38
4	Yankee Mon	$ 1,796	33
5	Organizer	$59,295	1
6	Seaside Salute	Carryover	0
7	Naughty New Yorker	$ 4,235	14
10	Galloping Grocer	$ 6,588	9
11	Carminooch	$11,859	5
12	Stevie Stressor	Carryover	0

West Virginia and Yankee Mon were 2.45-1 and 3.80-1, respectively, meaning they attracted a combined 43 percent of the win pool, but they accounted for 71 of the 104 live pick-six tickets, or 68 percent of them. At 9.20-1, Spite the Devil had 8.4 percent of the win pool but less than 3 percent of the pick-six action. Put another way, there was less than three times as much bet to win on Yankee Mon as on Spite the Devil, but 11 times as many live pick-six tickets to him.

In the pick six, and to a lesser extent in the pick four, a horse's ordinal rank in the betting can be as important as his actual odds. The public had ranked the six contenders the same way I had, essentially making West Virginia (2.45-1) and Yankee Mon (3.80-1) their A's, Galloping Grocer (4.60-1) and Naughty New Yorker (6.10-1) their B's, and Carminooch (8-1) and Spite the Devil (9.10-1) their C's. Few of them, however, had gone beyond their A's in the pick six and fewer still had gone five- or six-deep.

Spite the Devil was no better than my fifth or sixth choice in the race, and it's hard for me to imagine a single-ticket play under which I would have gone that deep in the Classic. By giving myself the chance to pick him up if everything else went well, though, I had gained the opportunity for a seriously overlaid payoff on a day when my biggest opinion had been that a couple of unexciting favorites would probably win.

If you can put yourself in that position a few times a year, it will work out for you sooner or later. In midstretch of the Classic, it didn't look good for sooner, as the unlikely Organizer splashed to a clear lead and seemed ready to make one bettor who had cast an even wider net than mine the lone winner at $59,295. Then someone came flying, and while it was hard to make out who it was in the rain and slop, it was Spite the Devil, surging in the final yards to win by a length. I hope the guy who was alive to Organizer was one of the two people with whom I shared the pool.

Feeling pretty pleased with myself, I jumped back into the pick six the next day despite the lack of a carryover, threw out the 4-5 shot who won the first leg by 10 1/4 lengths, and did not have more than two winners on any ticket. The game will keep you humble. But Showcase Day had emboldened me for the somewhat more important day of stakes racing the following Saturday at Belmont, the Breeders' Cup. I decided that $10,000 from my after-tax return of around $15,000 from Showcase Day would be my bankroll for the best day of exotic betting on the planet, with a third of it going to a pick six where the pool would be much closer to $5 million than $59,295.

TENTH RACE
Belmont
OCTOBER 22, 2005

1⅛ MILES. (1.45^{2}) 30TH RUNNING OF THE EMPIRE CLASSIC HANDICAP. Purse $250,000 A HANDICAP FOR THREE YEAR OLDS AND UPWARD FOALED IN NEW YORK STATE AND APPROVED BY THE NEW YORK STATE-BRED REGISTRY. By subscription of $250 each, which should accompany the nomination; $1,250 to pass the entry box and $1,250 to start. The purse to be divided 60% to the winner, 20% to second, 10% to third, 5% to fourth, 3% to fifth and 2% divided equally among remaining finishers. A trophy will be presented to the winning owner. Closed Saturday, October 8, 2005 with 18 Nominations.

Value of Race: $250,000 Winner $150,000; second $50,000; third $25,000; fourth $12,500; fifth $7,500; sixth $1,000; seventh $1,000; eighth $1,000; ninth $1,000; tenth $1,000. Mutuel Pool $540,886.00 Exacta Pool $418,347.00 Trifecta Pool $314,774.00 Superfecta Pool $122,696.00

Last Raced	Horse	M/Eqt.	A.	Wt	PP	St	¼	½	¾	Str	Fin	Jockey	Odds $1
11Jun05 ^{9}Bel^{8}	Spite the Devil	L b	5	119	1	9	9^{hd}	$8^{1\frac{1}{2}}$	$8^{1\frac{1}{2}}$	$3^{1\frac{1}{2}}$	1^{1}	Castellano J J	9.20
17Sep05 ^{4}Bel^{1}	Organizer	L f	3	115	5	4	$3^{1\frac{1}{2}}$	3^{1}	3^{2}	$1^{\frac{1}{2}}$	$2^{1\frac{1}{4}}$	Dominguez R A	13.30
18Sep05 ^{9}Bel^{7}	Carminooch	L	3	113	9	2	$7^{3\frac{1}{2}}$	$4^{\frac{1}{2}}$	$7^{1\frac{1}{2}}$	$4^{\frac{1}{2}}$	3^{nk}	Luzzi M J	8.00
9Sep05 ^{8}Bel^{3}	Yankee Mon	L	4	119	4	6	$1^{\frac{1}{2}}$	$1^{2\frac{1}{2}}$	1^{1}	$2^{1\frac{1}{2}}$	4^{6}	Prado E S	3.80
28Aug05 ^{9}Mth^{1}	West Virginia	L	4	120	3	7	$6^{1\frac{1}{2}}$	$6^{3\frac{1}{2}}$	$5^{1\frac{1}{2}}$	5^{6}	$5^{3\frac{1}{4}}$	Velazquez J R	2.45
30Sep05 ^{8}Med^{6}	NaughtyNewYorker	L b	3	114	7	10	10	9^{5}	9^{8}	$6^{2\frac{1}{2}}$	6^{6}	Samyn J L	6.10
20Sep05 ^{9}Pha^{2}	Stevie Stressor	L b	4	114	10	1	4^{1}	7^{2}	4^{hd}	8^{6}	$7^{3\frac{1}{4}}$	Fragoso P	67.50
3Aug05 ^{8}Sar^{2}	Galloping Grocer	L	3	115	8	3	$2^{1\frac{1}{2}}$	$2^{1\frac{1}{2}}$	$2^{\frac{1}{2}}$	7^{hd}	$8^{1\frac{1}{2}}$	Coa E M	4.70
21Aug05 ^{6}Sar^{1}	Runingforpresident	L	4	114	2	5	5^{2}	5^{hd}	6^{hd}	9^{15}	$9^{45\frac{3}{4}}$	Morales P	44.50
21Aug05 ^{3}Sar^{1}	Seaside Salute	L	4	114	6	8	$8^{\frac{1}{2}}$	10	10	10	10	Bailey J D	22.90

OFF AT 5:51 Start Good. Won driving. Track sloppy (Sealed).

TIME :22^{3}, :45^{3}, 1:10, 1:36^{3}, 1:50^{4} (:22.62, :45.61, 1:10.19, 1:36.66, 1:50.86)

$2 Mutuel Prices:				
	1 – SPITE THE DEVIL	20.40	11.80	7.00
	5 – ORGANIZER		12.60	7.90
	11 – CARMINOOCH			6.00

$2 EXACTA 1-5 PAID $296.00 $2 TRIFECTA 1-5-11 PAID $2,932.00
$2 SUPERFECTA 1-5-11-4 PAID $30,673.00

Dk. b or br. g, (Mar), by Devil His Due - Samantha D, by Cryptoclearance. Trainer Jerkens H Allen. Bred by Elisabeth R Jerkens (NY).

SPITE THE DEVIL was outrun early, rallied four wide on the turn, finished gamely outside and was clear under the wire, driving. ORGANIZER raced close up inside, came wide into the stretch, rallied to get the lead nearing the eighth pole, led into deep stretch and was caught nearing the finish. CARMINOOCH was urged along outside, dropped back on the turn then came again in the stretch. YANKEE MON was hustled to the front, set the pace along the inside and weakened on the rail in the stretch. WEST VIRGINIA was unhurried early, put in a four wide run on the turn and tired in the stretch. NAUGHTY NEW YORKER was outrun early, raced wide and had no response when roused. STEVIE STRESSOR tired after a half mile. GALLOPING GROCER chased the pace from the outside for three quarters and tired. RUNINGFORPRESIDENT raced close up along the inside and was finished after a half mile. SEASIDE SALUTE tired badly and was eased in the stretch.

Owners– 1, Hardwicke Stable; 2, Majesty Stud; 3, Three Amigos Stable; 4, Windmill Manor Farm; 5, Zuckerman Donald S and Roberta Mary; 6, Fox Ridge Farm Inc; 7, Blue Streak Stable; 8, Rosenthal Robert D and Waldbaum Bernice; 9, Anstu Stables Inc; 10, Castle Village Farm

Trainers– 1, Jerkens H Allen; 2, Galluscio Dominic G; 3, Pletcher Todd A; 4, Dutrow Richard E Jr; 5, Pletcher Todd A; 6, Kelly Patrick J; 7, Allard Edward T; 8, Schettino Dominick A; 9, Barbara Robert; 10, Turner William H Jr

Scratched– Raffit (05Sep05 ^{6}Sar^{1}), Mr. Determined (29Sep05 ^{3}Bel^{4})

$2 Daily Double (7–1) Paid $77.50; Daily Double Pool $215,578.
$2 Pick Three (8–7–1) Paid $569.00; Pick Three Pool $164,115.
$2 Pick Four (1–8–7–1) Paid $3,927.00; Pick Four Pool $243,532.
$2 Pick Six (12–1–1–8–7–1) 6 Correct Paid $19,765.00; Pick Six Pool $93,012.
$2 Pick Six (12–1–1–8–7–1) 5 Correct Paid $116.50.

Belmont Park Attendance: 7,333 Mutuel Pool: $1,190,455.00 ITW Mutuel Pool: $3,842,836.00 ISW Mutuel Pool: $8,544,501.00

7 BIG DAYS, BIG BETS

THERE ARE THREE main reasons why it is tougher to succeed at betting horses now than it was a generation ago. First, takeout has steadily increased, from 10 percent in the 1940's to 25 percent or higher in today's exotic pools. Second, the information and technology explosions of the last 20 years have given the average player access to previously scarce or proprietary information, such as speed figures, trainer statistics, lifetime past performances, and video replays.

The biggest factor, however, may be the gradual disappearance of the very worst horseplayers, who used to fatten the pools by betting virtually at random, on names, numbers, colors, jockeys, or harebrained systems. These action junkies have largely been wooed away from their former seats in racetrack grandstands by the superior customer service and amenities of casinos or the mega-jackpots of state lotteries.

The one glorious exception to this trend is the one glorious exception to racing's declining live attendance: the Big Event

Day. These have been steadily growing in popularity even as daily live business has plummeted. Six horses won both the Kentucky Derby and Preakness from 1997 through 2004, making the Triple Crown more popular than ever. Betting on the Breeders' Cup has increased fivefold in the last 20 years. The only race meetings showing steady annual growth are short, high-quality boutique meetings such as Saratoga, Del Mar, and Keeneland, due to their popularity with occasional, event-driven attendees.

Exotic betting intensifies the advantages presented by these special days. Many of the additional players will be attempting inappropriate pools for which they are badly underfunded, and the necessity of combining more than one correct opinion in exotic bets will cause weaker players to fail more often than they would in the straight pools alone. Also, there are special exotic pools on many of these days that are heavily promoted and will attract plenty of casual money.

The basic benefit of playing on these occasions is simply that a much higher percentage of the handle will be coming from uninformed and unsophisticated investors than on a rainy Thursday when the regulars are competing only with one another for any scraps of value. Special days attract three additional subgroups: weekend-only players, big-event-only players, and total novices.

The infusion of their money can only make things easier for the regular player and can do the same for the enthusiastic hobbyist willing to put some extra effort into these cards. Focusing on these days is a viable plan of attack for this latter group of players, who are never going to spend hours keeping detailed notes or performing obscure calculations of their own on midweek claiming races. However, they can regularly follow the top tier of stakes racing that dominates these days and come up with worthwhile opinions of their own. If you're only going to play 10 or 20 or 50 times a year, why not play the 10 or 20 or 50 days that have both the best racing *and* the best wagering opportunities?

This does not mean that the biggest race of the big days is necessarily the focal point, or that some of these races do not have serious drawbacks that can outweigh the value of the extra uninformed money being invested in them. The best example of this is the most famous race of all, the Kentucky Derby. If the Derby were the unheralded fifth race on a Wednesday afternoon, many regulars would dismiss it with a small action bet or pass it entirely. It is a race filled with uncertainty and randomness, and the same things that make it seductive also make it nearly unbettable: The horses are erratic and still developing, the distance is a new one for almost every starter, the oversized field is prone to traffic and bad trips. It is not the kind of race on which a sensible, regular horseplayer would want to stake his reputation, much less a sizeable chunk of his bankroll.

It also is a race that is thoroughly scrutinized by handicappers and sportswriters, leaving few exclusive perceptions. All of this additional public analysis is not necessarily particularly smart or insightful, but unlike most races, there is full reporting on every contestant, and every nugget of information in the past performances has probably been noticed and considered.

By contrast, though, every other race on the Derby card is underanalyzed by both the general press and the majority of the patrons. The typical casual handicapper planning to play the Derby Day card has probably spent literally an hour thinking about and looking at the Derby for every minute he has devoted to the other 10 or 11 races. The same is true, if not quite as pointedly so, on a dozen or more big days a year when a race such as the Santa Anita Handicap, Florida Derby, or Travers consumes everyone's time and attention at the expense of several preceding races on which millions of dollars are being bet but far less analytical time is being invested. Multirace bets can be especially rewarding on these days because of this sloppier handicapping on races preceding the main event.

One trap to avoid is thinking that you must come up with an esoteric idea in every one of these races, a mistake I used to make out of greediness in the face of all the money floating around on the big-event days. I would focus almost solely on 20-1 shots who had experienced subtly fascinating trips that 99.7 percent of my competition wouldn't possibly know about, and reflexively try to beat every boring, obvious favorite on the card. Only years of unhappy endings to these days ultimately convinced me that there's no point in opposing very likely winners just because even the most casual fan can come up with them too. The trick, as always, is to decide which races are as easy as they look and which ones aren't.

At the risk of sounding like a ruler-wielding schoolmarm, I cannot emphasize too strongly how important it is to do your homework before post time. Past performances are usually available three full days before these big days, but even if you start looking at the races and plotting your exotic tickets in earnest just the night before, you will have a serious edge on your competition. While everyone else is still flipping pages and scrawling out pick-something tickets while standing on a long, slow-moving betting line, or trying to get through on busy phone lines as post time nears, you can be making some final adjustments to a well thought out investment.

Make your multirace bets as early as you can on these days, not only to avoid being shut out, but also to free your time and attention for race-by-race vertical wagers where you will want to be paying close attention to the tote board for opportunities. This will also force you to adopt some bankroll discipline, in that you need to have enough of a stake for both your advance multirace wagers and to be able to play the races individually. Your success at the former should affect neither your funding nor your strategy for the latter, at least not until you are on the brink of a success and in a position where it makes sense to consider hedging.

Breeders' Cup Day 2005

Even without the unexpected Spite the Devil pick six a week earlier, the 2005 Breeders' Cup at Belmont would probably have been my highest-handle day of the year. While some of the Cup races are always as overexposed and nearly as impossible as the Kentucky Derby, the attraction of the biggest pick-six pool and the two biggest pick-four pools of the year is irresistible. The Showcase Day success only confirmed my resolve to get involved in as many of the day's exotic pools as possible and to take a major swing at the Breeders' Cup Ultra Pick Six.

The U.P.S. began in 1997, replacing an ill-conceived Breeders' Cup Pick 7 that had been offered from 1991 through 1996. Breeders' Cup races, which frequently draw full fields of 14, are tough enough that a pick six is more than sufficiently daunting without extending it to a seventh race. The Pick 7 drew $8.5 million the first year it was offered, but then dropped in popularity as players came to consider it simply an impossible proposition, attracting just $3.3 million in its final incarnation in 1996:

Year	Handle	Winners	Payoff	Consos	Conso Payoff
1991	$8,526,965	0	—	29	$230,250
1992	$5,104,480	4	$ 740,115	349	$ 2,800
1993	$5,307,815	2	$1,549,114	2,054	$ 510
1994	$4,599,918	0	—	54	$ 66,290
1995	$3,169,020	81	$ 22,513	2,959	$ 205
1996	$3,340,945	4	$ 471,812	141	$ 4,462

The pick seven was replaced by a more conventional pick six in 1997, and after a slow first year the bet eventually stabilized with an annual handle of right around $4.5 million:

Year	Handle	Winners	Payoff	Consos	Conso Payoff
1997	$3,379,014	115	$ 12,417	*	$ 158
1998	$6,494,193	114	$ 34,607	3,906	$ 335
1999	$5,436,691	1	$3,058,138	*	$ 5,996
2000	$5,123,453	68	$ 45,772	*	$ 465
2001	$4,811,450	11	$ 262,422	*	$ 1,475
2002	$4,569,515	0	—	78	$ 43,937
2003	$4,489,454	1	$2,687,611	48	$ 18,663
2004	$4,566,837	0	—	61	$ 56,149

(*Information unavailable. Note also that different takeout rates and different main-pool/consolation-pool splits apply in the different jurisdictions in which the Cup is run each year.)

Clearly, even reduced from seven to six races, this is an extraordinarily difficult bet. In four of its first eight years, there was either no winning ticket or just one. There would have been no winners for three straight years from 2002 through 2004 except that one player lucked into $2.7 million in 2003 by buying a single $8 ticket as a lark.

While the Ultra Pick Six has leveled off, Breeders' Cup pick fours have shown explosive growth. Introduced in 2000, the inaugural pick four on the card's last four races drew just $565,571, but that increased to $903,567 in 2001, $1.06 million in 2002, and $1.28 million in 2003. A second pick four, on the first four Cup races, was added in 2004 and it handled $1.03 million, with $1.46 million being bet on the late pick four.

The growing popularity of the pick four, as both an alternative and an addition to the pick six, was easy to understand. The $2 pick-four payoffs had seemed like pick sixes on a normal day, ranging from $1,627 to $46,791, and every sequence had involved some short-priced winners, with no more than two winners at double-digit odds. In the 2004 early pick four, Ashado ($6) and Sweet Catomine ($6.60) were favored, and Speightstown ($9.40) was a close second choice. Adding Singletary to the mix as the eighth choice at 16-1 made the payoff $3,130.20, roughly double the parlay of the win prices.

The 2004 late pick four comprising the Filly and Mare Turf, Juvenile, Turf, and Classic left many players kicking themselves for missing a gigantic payoff that looked less than impossible in retrospect. Many may have considered Ouija Board at 9-10 in the Filly and Mare Turf and Ghostzapper at 5-2 in the Classic very solid favorites, if not clear singles. A $1 pick-four play singling the two of them that also managed to come up with Wilko at 28-1 in the Juvenile and Better Talk Now at 27-1 in the Turf returned $46,791.20 for $2, better than four times the parlay.

For all those reasons, and because of a few strong opinions, I wanted to jump into all three pools in 2005—the pick six and the two pick fours. I decided to allot my Cup Day bankroll of $10,000 roughly as follows: about $3,600 to the pick six and $1,200 for each pick four, leaving me $4,000, or about $500 per race, for straight and intrarace bets on each of the eight individual Cup races.

Here was what the Breeders' Cup lineup looked like:

Race 3: Breeders' Cup Juvenile Fillies
Race 4: Breeders' Cup Juvenile
Race 5: Breeders' Cup Filly and Mare Turf
Race 6: Breeders' Cup Sprint
Race 7: Breeders' Cup Mile
Race 8: Breeders' Cup Distaff
Race 9: Breeders' Cup Turf
Race 10: Breeders' Cup Classic

My experience at every Breeders' Cup has been that the races whiz by so quickly that even more advance plotting and planning than usual is advisable. With a championship race every 30 minutes, long lines at the track, and year-high volume on account-wagering phone lines, I decided to put in all my multirace wagers for the day well before the third race, the Juvenile Fillies.

The two pick fours were on Races 3 through 6 and Races 7 through 10, with the pick six on Races 5 through 10, creating some overlap where a single bad idea could knock me out of two of three multirace pools for the day. The way the races were carded, this was a distinct possibility, because my strongest Breeders' Cup opinion involved one of those overlap races, the Sprint. It featured the day's heaviest favorite, Lost in the Fog, a horse I was going to try to beat. My two other firm opinions involved horses who would be lone A's later on, Leroidesanimaux in the Mile and Saint Liam in the Classic.

By the time I arrived at Belmont at 10:00 on Breeders' Cup morning, I had all 101 Cup horses broken down as A's, B's,

C's, or X's, and preliminary matrices for the three multirace ventures. It was far too cold to sit outside, so I found a piece of a bench in the clubhouse near the self-service betting machines to do my final computations. When the changes for the card were announced over the loudspeaker system, there were two important ones: In the Mile, Leroidesanimaux would be wearing a bar shoe, usually a sign of a foot problem. In the Classic, Rock Hard Ten, the second favorite, was a late scratch.

The latter change would only make my life easier, as Rock Hard Ten was one of only two B's I had planned to use behind Saint Liam, so I'd have either some extra money to spread around or an opportunity to elevate someone else from C to B status. The Leroidesanimaux announcement was more troublesome. At his best he was simply several lengths better than anyone he was running against, but now he might *not* be at his best. On the other hand, trainer Bobby Frankel wouldn't run him at all if he thought the foot problem was really serious, would he? If I changed an entire pick-six play that largely singled him and he won anyway, I would feel like an idiot for overvaluing the equipment change.

I decided to split the difference. I would play him as strongly in the pick six as I had planned to, since doing otherwise would necessitate an entire change of strategy, but in the late pick four I would spread out in the Mile. Assuming I got through the first two legs of the pick six, then I would still be leaning heavily on Leroidesanimaux in that pool, but if he lost I'd probably be in decent pick-four position by having started out by beating a heavy favorite—a compromise born of indecision.

Once I had everything worked out, I walked to a self-service machine while the first race was being run and settled in for what turned out to be 19 minutes of punching out 25 separate pick-four and pick-six tickets. (It was too noisy to put my tickets in over the phone.) Every time someone walked up behind me to form a line, I turned around and said, "Sorry, I'm going to be awhile," and the lines weren't too bad, since it was only the second race of the day. Had I tried tying up a self-service machine for 19 minutes later on, there might have been fisticuffs.

For the record, here were the plays:

EARLY PICK FOUR				
Race	A Horses	B Horses	C Horses	X Horses
3rd	1,7	2,5,6	—	3,4,8,9,10
4th	8,9,12,14	—	—	1,2,3,4,5,6,7,10,11,13
5th	5,7,13	2,4,12	8,9,14	1,3,6,10,11
6th	1,5,6,11	—	3,4,7,8,10	2,9

Ticket	Array	Details	Combos/Unit		Cost
1.	AAAA	1,7/8,9,12,14/5,7,13/1,5,6,11	96 @ $5	= $	480
2.	BAAA	2,5,6/8,9,12,14/5,7,13/1,5,6,11	144 @ $2	= $	288
3.	AABA	1,7/8,9,12,14/2,4,12/1,5,6,11	96 @ $2	= $	192
4.	BABA	2,5,6/8,9,12,14/2,4,12/1,5,6,11	144 @ $1	= $	144
5.	AACA	1,7/8,9,12,14/8,9,14/1,5,6,11	96 @ $1	= $	96
6.	AAAC	1,7/8,9,12,14/5,7,13/3,4,7,8,10	120@ $1	= $	120
			TOTAL	= $	1,320

PICK SIX				
Race	**A Horses**	**B Horses**	**C Horses**	**X Horses**
5th	5,7,13	2,4,12	8,9,14	1,3,6,10,11
6th	1,5,6,11	—	3,4,7,8,10	2,9
7th	11	—	2,3,8,9,10,12	1,4,5,6,7
8th	3,7,11	—	1,9,10	2,4,5,6,8,12,13
9th	3,5	2,4	6,7,10,13	1,8,9,11,12
10th	13	11	3,5,8,9	2,4,6,7,10,12,14

Ticket	**Array**	**Details**	**Cost**
1.	All A+B	2,4,5,7,12,13/1,5,6,11/11/3,7,11/2,3,4,5/11,13	= $ 1,152
2.	CAAAAA	8,9,14/1,5,6,11/11/3,7,11/3,5/13	= $ 144
3.	ACAAAA	5,7,13/3,4,7,8,10/11/3,7,11/3,5/13	= $ 180
4.	AACAAA	5,7,13/1,5,6,11/2,3,8,9,10,12/3,7,11/3,5/13	= $ 864
5.	AAACAA	5,7,13/1,5,6,11/11/1,9,10/3,5/13	= $ 144
6.	AAAACA	5,7,13/1,5,6,11/11/3,7,11/6,7,10,13/13	= $ 288
7.	AAAAAC	5,7,13/1,5,6,11/11/3,7,11/3,5/3,5,8,9	= $ 576
		Total	= $3,348

(Note: Rather than do the usual permutations that would have allowed only two of my B's to win, and given that my head was already spinning with tickets and numbers, I bought a primary ticket with all my A's and B's, which added only $144 to my total cost and saved me the possible horror of zigzagging out of millions with three A's and three B's.)

LATE PICK FOUR				
Race	A Horses	B Horses	C Horses	X Horses
7th	9,10,11	2,3,8,12	1,4,5,6,7	—
8th	3,7,11	—	1,9,10	2,4,5,6,8,12,13
9th	3,5	2,4,7,13	6,10	1,8,9,11,12
10th	13	3,11	4,5,8,9,14	2,6,7,10,12

Ticket	Array	Details	Combos/Unit	Cost
1.	AAAA	9,10,11/3,7,11/3,5/13	18 @ $10	= $ 180
2.	BAAA	2,3,8,12/3,7,11/3,5/13	24 @ $ 5	= $ 120
3.	AABA	9,10,11/3,7,11/2,4,7,13/13	36 @ $ 5	= $ 180
4.	AAAB	9,10,11/3,7,11/3,5/3,11	36 @ $ 5	= $ 180
5.	BABA	2,3,8,12/3,7,11/2,4,7,13/13	48 @ $ 1	= $ 48
6.	BAAB	2,3,8,12/3,7,11/3,5/3,11	48 @ $ 1	= $ 48
7.	AABB	9,10,11/3,7,11/2,4,7,13/3,11	72 @ $ 1	= $ 72
8.	BABB	2,3,8,12/3,7,11/2,4,7,13/3,11	96 @ $ 1	= $ 96
9.	CAAA	1,4,5,6,7/3,7,11/3,5/13	30 @ $ 1	= $ 30
10.	ACAA	9,10,11/1,9,10/3,5/13	18 @ $ 1	= $ 18
11.	AACA	9,10,11/3,7,11/6,10/13	18 @ $ 1	= $ 18
12.	AAAC	9,10,11/3,7,11/3,5/4,5,8,9,14	90 @ $ 1	= $ 90

TOTAL = $1,080

The primary difference between the pick-six and late pick-four plays was changing my approach to the Mile from one A and six C's to three A's and four B's. In addition, I elevated all my X horses from the Mile to C's, and two of my four Turf C's to B's.

Having put $1,320 into the early pick four, $3,348 into the pick six, and $1,080 into the late pick four, my account balance was now $5,748 lighter than it had been 19 minutes earlier, and it was still an hour until the first Breeders' Cup race.

THIRD RACE
Belmont
OCTOBER 29, 2005

1 1/16 MILES. (1.39²) 22ND RUNNING OF THE ALBERTO V05 BREEDERS' CUP JUVENILE FILLIES. Grade I. Purse $1,000,000 FOR FILLIES, TWO–YEAR–OLDS. Weight 119 lbs. $10,000 to pre–enter, $20,000 to enter, with guaranteed $1 million purse including nominator awards (plus Net Supplementary Fees, if any), of which 52% of all monies to the owner of the winner, 20% to second, 11% to third, 5.7% to fourth and 3% to fifth; plus stallion nominator awards of 2.6% of all monies to the winner, 1% to second and 0.55% to third and foal nominator awards of 2.6% of all monies to the winner, 1% to second and 0.55% to third. Closed with 14pre–entries. Supplemental Nominee: Wild Fit.

Value of Race: $972,020 Winner $551,200; second $212,000; third $116,600; fourth $60,420; fifth $31,800. Mutuel Pool $3,329,694.00 Exacta Pool $2,502,872.00 Trifecta Pool $2,070,537.00 Head2Head Pool $50,957.00 Superfecta Pool $621,890.00

Last Raced	Horse	M/Eqt.	A.	Wt	PP	St	1/4	1/2	3/4	Str	Fin	Jockey	Odds $1
17Sep05 8Bel¹	Folklore	L	2	119	1	4	1½	2½	2½	1³	1¹¼	Prado E S	2.35
10ct05 4OSA²	Wild Fit	L	2	119	10	10	10	10	9²	4ʰᵈ	2⁴¾	Solis A	7.00
18Sep05 7AP¹	Original Spin	L b	2	119	2	8	7½	4ʰᵈ	3¹½	3¹	3ʰᵈ	Bailey J D	4.30
70ct05 9Kee²	Ex Caelis	L	2	119	9	3	9⁶	9⁴	5¹	2ʰᵈ	4³	Bejarano R	16.70
20ct05 7Bel¹	Sensation	L	2	119	7	2	8ʰᵈ	8ʰᵈ	6½	6²	5³¼	Coa E M	11.40
10ct05 6WO¹	Knights Templar	L	2	119	5	5	2½	1ʰᵈ	1ʰᵈ	5¹½	6³¼	Stevens G L	8.90
80ct05 8Bel¹	Adieu	L	2	119	6	1	3ʰᵈ	5¹	7¹	8¹	76¼	Velazquez J R	4.20
80ct05 8Bel²	Along the Sea	L b	2	119	3	6	4½	3ʰᵈ	4½	72½	82¼	Castellano J J	22.90
70ct05 9Kee¹	She Says It Best	L	2	119	8	7	5¹	6¹	8½	10	9²	Martin E M Jr	27.25
10ct05 4OSA¹	Diamond Omi	L	2	119	4	9	6ʰᵈ	7½	10	9½	10	Espinoza V	19.60

OFF AT 1:22 Start Good. Won driving. Track fast.

TIME :22³, :45¹, 1:10¹, 1:36⁴, 1:43⁴ (:22.65, :45.34, 1:10.39, 1:36.81, 1:43.85)

$2 Mutuel Prices:

1 – FOLKLORE	6.70	4.20	2.70
10 – WILD FIT		6.40	4.30
2 – ORIGINAL SPIN			3.70

$2 EXACTA 1–10 PAID $54.50 $2 TRIFECTA 1–10–2 PAID $181.50
$2 HEAD2HEAD 4VS.9WINNER9 PAID $3.40
$2 SUPERFECTA 1–10–2–9 PAID $1,762.00

B. f, (Feb), by Tiznow – Contrive , by Storm Cat . Trainer Lukas D Wayne. Bred by Robert Lewis & Beverly Lewis (Ky).

Folklore's victory as the favorite in the Breeders' Cup Juvenile Fillies was my second-best result for the early pick four, as she and Sensation at 11-1 had been my two A's. I hadn't used the runner-up, Wild Fit, at all, so I felt as if I had dodged a bullet.

I made my first non-exotic bet of the day half an hour later in the Juvenile, where I had used four A's in equal strength: First Samurai at 6-5, Stevie Wonderboy at 9-2, Sorceror's Stone at 7-1, and Dr. Pleasure at 44-1. At that price, I had to do something more with Dr. Pleasure than just root for him in the pick four, so I bet $200 to win and took him back and forth in $20 exactas with my other three A's. Also, I confess, I wheeled him back and forth with "all" in $1 exactas, just in case he ran second to some other bomb. (On second thought, I should have only back-wheeled him to run second in the exacta, given that I was perfectly well covered with both a win bet and in pick fours, so that was $13 poorly spent.) In any case, Dr. Pleasure ran an indifferent seventh, and Stevie Wonderboy kept me alive.

FOURTH RACE
Belmont
OCTOBER 29, 2005

$1\frac{1}{16}$ MILES. (1.39^{2}) 22ND RUNNING OF THE BESSEMER TRUST BREEDERS' CUP JUVENILE. Grade I. Purse $1,500,000 FOR COLTS AND GELDINGS, TWO YEARS OLD. Weight, 122 lbs. $15,000 to pre-enter, $30,000 to enter, with guaranteed $1.5 million purse including nominator awards (plus Net Supplementary Fees, if any), of which 52% of all monies to the owner of the winner, 20% to second,11% to third, 5.7% to fourth and 3% to fifth; plus stallion nominator awards of 2.6% of all monies to the winner, 1% to second and 0.55% to third and foal nominator awards of 2.6% of all monies to the winner, 1% to second and 0.55% to third. Closed with 17 pre-entries. Supplemental nominee: Jealous Profit.

Value of Race: $1,458,030 Winner $826,800; second $318,000; third $174,900; fourth $90,630; fifth $47,700. Mutuel Pool $4,157,292.00 Exacta Pool $3,047,118.00 Trifecta Pool $2,549,902.00 Head2Head Pool $59,014.00 Superfecta Pool $922,589.00

Last Raced	Horse	M/Eqt.	A.	Wt	PP	St	¼	½	¾	Str	Fin	Jockey	Odds $1
7Sep05 ^{8}Dmr^{1}	Stevie Wonderboy	L	2	122	12	9	$12^{2\frac{1}{2}}$	11^{hd}	$5^{\frac{1}{2}}$	3^{3}	$1^{1\frac{1}{4}}$	Gomez G K	4.50
8Oct05 ^{9}Bel^{2}	Henny Hughes	L	2	122	10	3	$2^{\frac{1}{2}}$	2^{hd}	1^{1}	1^{1}	2^{2}	Prado E S	9.30
8Oct05 ^{9}Bel^{1}	First Samurai	L	2	122	9	10	9^{1}	8^{hd}	$3^{\frac{1}{2}}$	$2^{1\frac{1}{2}}$	$3^{5\frac{1}{4}}$	Bailey J D	1.30
2Oct05 ^{6}OSA^{1}	Brother Derek	L	2	122	13	2	4^{hd}	4^{hd}	2^{hd}	$4^{\frac{1}{2}}$	4no	Solis A	56.75
8Oct05 ^{9}Bel^{3}	Superfly	L	2	122	1	13	13^{2}	10^{hd}	$8^{\frac{1}{2}}$	$5^{1\frac{1}{2}}$	$5^{3\frac{1}{4}}$	Coa E M	48.50
18Sep05 ^{9}AP^{1}	Sorcerer's Stone	L b	2	122	8	6	5^{hd}	9^{2}	6^{hd}	$6^{2\frac{1}{2}}$	$6^{1\frac{1}{4}}$	Guidry M	7.70
2Oct05 ^{8}Bel^{2}	Dr. Pleasure	L	2	122	14	1	$8^{\frac{1}{2}}$	$13^{2\frac{1}{2}}$	13^{2}	10^{1}	$7^{2\frac{1}{2}}$	Santos J A	44.50
8Oct05 ^{8}Kee^{3}	Stream Cat	b	2	122	7	14	14	14	$12^{1\frac{1}{2}}$	9^{hd}	$8^{1\frac{1}{2}}$	Stevens G L	22.60
25Sep05 NEW^{1}	Leo-GB		2	122	3	11	10^{hd}	6^{hd}	10^{hd}	7^{hd}	$9^{2\frac{1}{4}}$	Dettori L	36.00
2Oct05 ^{6}OSA^{3}	Jealous Profit	L b	2	122	5	8	7^{hd}	7^{hd}	$9^{1\frac{1}{2}}$	8^{1}	$10^{17\frac{1}{4}}$	Nakatani C S	62.25
8Oct05 ^{8}Kee^{1}	Dawn of War	L	2	122	6	4	$1^{\frac{1}{2}}$	$1^{\frac{1}{2}}$	4^{1}	11^{6}	$11^{1\frac{1}{2}}$	Castellano J J	32.50
30Sep05 NEW^{4}	Ivan Denisovich-Ire	L	2	122	2	12	$11^{\frac{1}{2}}$	12^{hd}	14	14	12^{1}	Fallon K	16.40
8Oct05 STC^{1}	Set Alight		2	122	4	7	$6^{\frac{1}{2}}$	$5^{1\frac{1}{2}}$	$11^{1\frac{1}{2}}$	$13^{\frac{1}{2}}$	13^{3}	Bejarano R	41.00
17Sep05 ^{9}Bel^{1}	Private Vow	L	2	122	11	5	3^{1}	3^{1}	7^{hd}	$12^{1\frac{1}{2}}$	14	Velazquez J R	10.30

OFF AT 2:01 Start Good. Won driving. Track fast.

TIME :23, $:45^{3}$, $1:10^{3}$, $1:35^{1}$, $1:41^{3}$ (:23.14, :45.75, 1:10.61, 1:35.34, 1:41.64)

$2 Mutuel Prices:				
	12 – STEVIE WONDERBOY	11.00	5.90	3.80
	10 – HENNY HUGHES		8.80	4.90
	9 – FIRST SAMURAI			2.50

$2 EXACTA 12–10 PAID $105.50 $2 TRIFECTA 12–10–9 PAID $229.00
$2 HEAD2HEAD 7VS.8VS.12WINNER12 PAID $4.00
$2 SUPERFECTA 12–10–9–13 PAID $7,051.00

Ch. c, (Mar), by Stephen Got Even – Heat Lightning , by Summer Squall . Trainer O'Neill Doug. Bred by John Gunther Tony Holmes & Walter Zent (Ky).

It was time for the pick six to begin with the Breeders' Cup Filly and Mare Turf, and I settled in to root for the longer prices among the 9 out of 14 fillies I had covered in both the pick four and pick six—three A's, three B's, and three C's. Obviously I didn't have much of a handle on the race, since I had used more than half the field, but the idea was just to get through it and then beat Lost in the Fog. With an A-A start in the early pick four, I was still alive on the $5 ticket ending A-A, for $2 on the ticket ending B-A, and for $1 on either a C-A or A-C finish. The only thing that could stop me in either the pick four or the pick six was a victory here by Luas Line, Sundrop, Flip Flop, Intercontinental, or Mona Lisa.

FIFTH RACE
Belmont
OCTOBER 29, 2005

1¼ MILES. (Inner Turf) (1.57^{3}) 7TH RUNNING OF THE EMIRATES AIRLINE BREEDERS' CUP FILLY&MARE TURF. Grade I. Purse $1,000,000 FOR FILLIES AND MARES, THREE-YEAR-OLDS AND UPWARD. Northern Hemisphere Three-Year-Olds, 119 lbs.; Older, 123 lbs. Southern Hemisphere Three-Year-Olds, 114 lbs.; Older, 123 lbs. $10,000 to pre-enter, $20,000 to enter, with guaranteed $1 million purse including nominator awards (plus Net Supplementary Fees, if any), of which 52% of all monies to the owner of the winner, 20% to second, 11% to third, 5.7% to fourth and 3% to fifth; plus stallion nominator awards of 2.6% of all monies to the winner, 1% to second and 0.55% to third and foal nominator awards of 2.6% of all monies to the winner, 1% to second and 0.55% to third. Closed with 14 pre-entries. Supplemental nominee: Flip Flop (Fr).

Value of Race: $972,020 Winner $551,200; second $212,000; third $116,600; fourth $60,420; fifth $31,800. Mutuel Pool $4,306,394.00 Exacta Pool $3,120,044.00 Trifecta Pool $2,550,499.00 Head2Head Pool $47,802.00 Superfecta Pool $827,125.00

Last Raced	Horse	M/Eqt.	A.	Wt	PP	¼	½	¾	1	Str	Fin	Jockey	Odds $1
9Oct05 ^{6}Kee^{1}	Intercontinentl-GB	L	5	123	10	1½	1^{2}	1½	1^{3}	1^{3}½	1^{1}¼	Bejarano R	15.10
24Sep05 ^{6}NEW^{1}	Ouija Board-GB	L	4	123	13	8^{hd}	7^{hd}	6½	2^{hd}	2½	2^{nk}	Bailey J D	2.30
1Oct05 ^{10}Bel^{3}	Film Maker	L b	5	123	2	11^{2}½	11^{1}	8½	4^{2}	3^{5}	3^{4}	Valenzuela P A	9.10
1Oct05 ^{10}Bel^{2}	Wonder Again	L	6	123	7	9^{1}	10½	10^{hd}	5^{hd}	4½	4^{2}	Prado E S	5.00
1Oct05 NEW^{8}	FvourbleTerms-GB		5	123	9	12^{2}½	12^{2}½	12^{2}	8½	6^{hd}	5^{1}	Kinane M J	28.75
9Oct05 ^{6}Kee^{2}	Wend	L	4	123	5	2^{1}	2^{1}	2½	3½	5^{1}	6^{nk}	Velazquez J R	12.70
1Oct05 ^{10}Bel^{9}	Angara-GB	L	4	123	14	13^{6}	13^{8}	13^{6}	13^{5}	7^{5}½	7^{4}¾	Stevens G L	29.50
1Oct05 ^{8}OSA^{1}	Megahertz-GB	L	6	123	8	14	14	14	14	14	8^{1}½	Solis A	5.00
15Oct05 ^{9}Kee^{2}	Karen's Caper	L	3	119	12	6½	6½	3½	6^{1}	8^{1}	9^{2}¾	Albarado R J	17.50
2Oct05 ^{8}LCH^{2}	Mona Lisa-GB	L	3	119	11	4½	3½	4^{hd}	10½	10^{2}	10¾	Fallon K	19.10
15Oct05 ^{9}Kee^{6}	Luas Line-Ire	L	3	119	1	10^{hd}	9^{hd}	7^{hd}	12½	12½	11^{5}½	Soumillon C	31.00
1Oct05 ^{8}OSA^{2}	Flip Flop-FR	L	4	123	6	5½	5^{hd}	5^{1}	9½	13^{hd}	12^{7}¼	Gomez G K	34.00
1Oct05 ^{10}Bel^{1}	Riskaverse	L	6	123	4	3^{hd}	4½	9^{hd}	11½	11½	13^{6}¼	Santos J A	20.20
1Oct05 ^{10}Bel^{5}	Sundrop-Jpn	L f	4	123	3	7^{hd}	8^{hd}	11^{2}½	7½	9^{1}	14	Dettori L	38.25

OFF AT 2:40 Start Good. Won driving. Course good.

TIME :24, :48^{4}, 1:13^{3}, 1:38, 2:02^{1} (:24.10, :48.92, 1:13.62, 1:38.17, 2:02.34)

$2 Mutuel Prices:				
	10 – INTERCONTINENTAL-GB	32.20	13.00	8.40
	13 – OUIJA BOARD-GB		5.90	4.30
	2 – FILM MAKER			6.40

$2 EXACTA 10–13 PAID $131.50 $2 TRIFECTA 10–13–2 PAID $1,167.00
$2 HEAD2HEAD 2VS.7VS.13WINNER13 PAID $4.60
$2 SUPERFECTA 10–13–2–7 PAID $5,004.00

B. m, (Mar), by Danehill – Hasili-Ire , by Kahyasi-Ire . Trainer Frankel Robert. Bred by Juddmonte Farms (GB).

Oops.

A year earlier, Intercontinental had been one of my favorite horses, a fiery filly with a strong late kick, but she had seemed to lose her punch since then and had turned into an intractable front-runner who had looked unlikely to go all the way at a mile and a quarter, farther than she had ever raced. In a race where everyone's best efforts were so close together, I had whittled away only those who looked abjectly overmatched or unlikely to handle the distance, and she had been one of them.

It took me a moment to realize the enormity of her victory and the extent of my deadness. I was out of the early pick four entirely and dead after exactly one leg of the year's biggest pick six. It made me feel only slightly better when I found out later that the AmeriTab Players' Pool, a syndicate that sells fractional interests in huge pick-six investments to the public for major events, had invested $93,212 in the pick six, had also gone nine-deep in the race, and had also left out Intercontinental.

The only good news was that it was under half an hour until the Sprint, and there was still money to be made beating Lost in the Fog, who had opened up as the 1-2 favorite, an absurd price for a horse I truly believed was well under 50 percent to win the race. Maybe I could beat him, be smart the rest of the way, and still collect some healthy pick-six consolations. After all, I could have as many as nine of them, one for each of my fillies who had failed to catch Intercontinental.

I had decided that this was the race where I would make my personal Breeders' Cup superfecta debut, because I thought that Lost in the Fog was a prime candidate not only to lose but also to finish off the board entirely. Lost in the Fog, a front-running 3-year-old sprinter, had become a national darling and the focus of much of the Breeders' Cup coverage. He was undefeated in 10 career starts and had admirably crisscrossed the country running in the handful of rich sprint stakes restricted to 3-year-olds.

His record seemed unassailable until you looked at it more analytically. In addition to running against suspect competition, he had been getting loose on the lead through slow fractions in most of his victories, but now he was going to face some serious early pressure from veteran older horses for the first time. If challenged early, he might wilt entirely, setting up an all-closers finish and a massive superfecta.

The question was how to structure the ticket. Should I

make a big box leaving out Lost in the Fog and the other front-runners who would burn out from chasing him, or key my top pick, Taste of Paradise (number 1), on a widening part-wheel using everybody for fourth? I chose the former, then went back and pressed Taste of Paradise running 1-2 with the other closers. With five minutes to post, I even bet $500 to win on Taste of Paradise, who was sitting at what I considered an astoundingly juicy 12-1. As the field went into the gate, I was holding the following tickets:

$1 superfecta box 1,3,5,6,8,10,11	= $840
$1 super 1/3,5,6,8,10,11/3,5,6,8,10,11/3,5,6,8,10,11	= $120
$1 super 3,5,6,8,10,11/1/3,5,6,8,10,11/3,5,6,8,10,11	= $120
$500 win, #1	= $500

With 50 yards to go, I was counting my riches. Lost in the Fog had cracked under pressure and the cavalry was coming. Taste of Paradise was in gear and moving fastest of all after briefly checking while waiting for room. It looked like I would collect $6,500 on the win bet and would have $2 worth of a superfecta that had to be paying $10,000 or better. What a great game.

Then two things happened at the wire. First, Taste of Paradise appeared to fall just short of catching Silver Train. So much for the win bet, but so what? A superfecta headed by an 11-1 and a 12-1 shot with the 7-10 favorite out of the money was still going to be enormous. That looked like Lion Tamer, another one of my A's, getting up for third over someone. As long as that someone wasn't Attila's Storm, Lifestyle, or Battle Won, I had it.

SIXTH RACE
Belmont
OCTOBER 29, 2005

6 FURLONGS. (1.07³) 22ND RUNNING OF THE TVG BREEDERS' CUP SPRINT. Grade I. Purse $1,000,000 FOR THREE–YEAR–OLDS AND UPWARD. Northern Hemisphere Three-Year-Olds, 124 lbs.; Older, 126 lbs.; Southern Hemisphere Three-Year-Olds, 122 lbs.; Older, 126 lbs. All Fillies and Mares allowed 3 lbs. $10,000 to pre–enter, $20,000 to enter, with guaranteed $1 million purse including nominator awards (plus Net Supplementary Fees, if any), of which 52% of all monies to the owner of the winner, 20% to second, 11% to third, 5.7% to fourth and 3% to fifth; plus stallion nominator awards of 2.6% of all monies to the winner, 1% to second and 0.55% to third and foal nominator awards of 2.6% of all monies to the winner, 1% to second and 0.55% to third. Closed with 14 pre–entries. Supplemental nominee: Lost in the Fog.

Value of Race: $972,020 Winner $551,200; second $212,000; third $116,600; fourth $60,420; fifth $31,800. Mutuel Pool $4,302,323.00 Exacta Pool $3,306,841.00 Trifecta Pool $2,895,076.00 Head2Head Pool $61,807.00 Superfecta Pool $1,120,360.00

Last Raced	Horse	M/Eqt. A. Wt	PP	St	¼	½	Str	Fin	Jockey	Odds $1
11Sep05 7Bel¹	Silver Train	L 3 124	3	2	5¹	5¹½	2ʰᵈ	1ʰᵈ	Prado E S	11.90
10ct05 6Bel¹	Taste of Paradise	L b 6 126	1	6	8¹½	7½	4¹	2³	Gomez G K	12.50
10ct05 6Bel³	Lion Tamer	L 5 126	5	10	9½	8²	5½	3ⁿᵏ	Velazquez J R	12.40
8Sep05 8Mth¹	Attila's Storm	L b 3 124	2	1	1½	2¹	3¹½	4²	Valenzuela P A	45.50
80ct05 6Kee¹	Elusive Jazz	L f 4 126	8	7	6³	6½	6²	5ʰᵈ	Albarado R J	53.50
21Aug05 2Dmr²	Lifestyle	L bf 5 126	9	9	10²	9¹½	7ʰᵈ	6½	Solis A	55.25
10ct05 8BM¹	Lost in the Fog	L 3 124	7	3	4²½	1½	1ʰᵈ	7½	Baze R A	0.70
10ct05 9Bel⁵	Imperialism	L b 4 126	10	11	11¹	11	9ʰᵈ	8³½	Espinoza V	19.50
23Sep05 7Bel¹	Gygistar	L 6 126	11	8	7½	10²	10¹	9⁵¾	Castellano J J	14.20
7Aug05 7Mth¹	Wildcat Heir	L f 5 126	6	4	3ʰᵈ	3½	8²	10²¾	Elliott S	6.40
90ct05 4Kee⁵	Battle Won	L 5 126	4	5	2ʰᵈ	4ʰᵈ	11	11	Dominguez R A	16.30

OFF AT 3:15 Start Good. Won driving. Track fast.
TIME :22, :44², :56³, 1:08⁴ (:22.01, :44.56, :56.65, 1:08.86)

$2 Mutuel Prices:

3 – SILVER TRAIN	25.80	10.40	8.10
1 – TASTE OF PARADISE		10.60	7.20
5 – LION TAMER			7.60

$2 EXACTA 3–1 PAID $215.50 $2 TRIFECTA 3–1–5 PAID $1,593.00
$2 HEAD2HEAD 3VS.5WINNER3 PAID $3.90
$2 SUPERFECTA 3–1–5–2 PAID $35,358.00

Dk. b or br. c, (Feb), by Old Trieste – Ridden in Thestars , by Cormorant . Trainer Dutrow Richard E Jr. Bred by Joe Mulholland Sr Joe Mulholland Jr et al (Ky).

Oops again, and I guess this is why I'm still a rare participant in superfectas. Attila's Storm would have been my 10th or 11th choice in the field of 11—a secondary speed horse who was sure to fade to the rear if the contested pace I was hoping for had developed. It had, and Attila's Storm had simply run an amazing race to be the only pace horse still close at the finish, nearly holding third while beaten less than 3½ lengths.

Everything else had gone perfectly. I had gotten Lost in the Fog off the board, I had gotten closers to run 1-2-3, and Taste of Paradise had run as well as you could ask without winning. Yet I was collecting nothing. My brain began to whine: Why hadn't I bet Taste of Paradise to win *and* place? Why hadn't I also boxed my seven horses in the trifecta, or keyed Taste of Paradise back and forth with the other closers in exactas? Why hadn't I hit the "all" button for fourth in my superfecta part-wheels?

It was one of those supreme moments of exotic-bettor's remorse, but decades of suffering such disappointments at least makes them go away quickly. There is always another way you could have played the race that would have worked out better. All you can do is try to learn something if there is indeed a lesson in defeat, turn the page, and move on.

But wait. It's never over until it's official, and suddenly the word that started blinking on the Belmont tote board was *Inquiry*. Taste of Paradise's rider, Garrett Gomez, was claiming foul against Silver Train. Perhaps the win bet was still good for something. Unfortunately, the replay clearly showed that while Taste of Paradise may have been unlucky to lose, it wasn't Silver Train's fault. The stewards did the right thing and left the result alone.

I was now stuck $6,594 for the day, not including the $1,080 I had put into the late pick four that was about to begin with the Mile. It occurred to me that only 50 percent of the Cup races had been run but I was already 65.94 percent of the way to my first five-digit losing day in 28 years of betting on horses.

Race	Bet Type	Bet	Return
3rd	Pick Four	$ 1,320	$ 0
4th	Win	$ 200	$ 0
4th	Exacta	$ 146	$ 0
5th	Pick Six	$ 3,348	$ 0
6th	Win	$ 500	$ 0
6th	Superfecta	$ 1,080	$ 0
Total		$ 6,594	$ 0

The only good news was that I couldn't get knocked out of the late pick four in the first leg, with three A's, four B's, and the other five starters as C's. A victory by Leroidesanimaux at 6-5 would be an uninteresting way to start things off, but at least would technically keep me alive for pick-six consos. Probably my worst result would be Artie Schiller, the second choice at 5-1 and the only one of the four favorites who was not an A in my pick fours.

SEVENTH RACE
Belmont
OCTOBER 29, 2005

1 MILE. (Turf) (1.31^{3}) 22ND RUNNING OF THE NETJETS BREEDERS' CUP MILE. Grade I. Purse $1,500,000 FOR THREE-YEAR-OLDS AND UPWARD. Northern Hemisphere Three-Year-Olds, 123 lbs.; Older, 126 lbs. Southern Hemisphere Three-Year-Olds, 120 lbs.; Older, 126 lbs. All Fillies and Mares allowed 3 lbs. $15,000 to pre-enter, $30,000 to enter, with guaranteed $1.5 million purse including nominator awards (plus Net Supplementary Fees, if any), of which 52% of all monies to the owner of the winner, 20% to second, 11% to third, 5.7% to fourth and 3% to fifth; plus stallion nominator awards of 2.6% of all monies to the winner, 1% to second and 0.55% to third and foal nominator awards of 2.6% of all monies to the winner, 1% to second and 0.55% to third. Closed with 16 pre-entries. Supplemental nominees: Host (Chi), Majors Cast (Ire), Gorella (Fr) and Leroidesanimaux (Brz).

Value of Race: $1,856,925 Winner $1,053,000; second $405,000; third $222,750; fourth $115,425; fifth $60,750. Mutuel Pool $4,539,066.00 Exacta Pool $3,236,724.00 Trifecta Pool $2,796,636.00 Head2Head Pool $46,074.00 Superfecta Pool $941,161.00

Last Raced	Horse	M/Eqt.	A.	Wt	PP	St	¼	½	¾	Str	Fin	Jockey	Odds $1
2Oct05 ^{9}Bel^{2}	Artie Schiller	L	4	126	2	10	5^{1}	$5\frac{1}{2}$	4^{1}	2^{hd}	$1\frac{3}{4}$	Gomez G K	5.60
18Sep05 ^{9}WO^{1}	Leroidesnimux-Brz	L	5	126	11	2	$3^{2\frac{1}{2}}$	$3^{2\frac{1}{2}}$	2^{1}	$1\frac{1}{2}$	2no	Velazquez J R	1.35
15Oct05 ^{9}Kee^{3}	Gorella-FR	L	3	120	8	8	$10^{4\frac{1}{2}}$	9^{1}	7^{1}	$5\frac{1}{2}$	3^{hd}	Stevens G L	13.70
4Sep05 ^{4}LCH^{4}	Whipper		4	126	3	9	7^{3}	7^{1}	5^{hd}	9^{7}	4^{1}	Murtagh J P	17.50
4Sep05 LCH^{3}	Majors Cast-Ire	L	4	126	7	7	$8\frac{1}{2}$	$8\frac{1}{2}$	$8\frac{1}{2}$	$7\frac{1}{2}$	$5\frac{1}{2}$	Dettori L	20.20
2Oct05 ^{9}Bel^{5}	Limehouse	L	4	126	12	3	$6\frac{1}{2}$	$6\frac{1}{2}$	$6\frac{1}{2}$	4^{hd}	$6\frac{1}{2}$	Santos J A	36.25
8Oct05 ^{9}Kee^{1}	Host-Chi	L	5	126	1	12	11	11	$10\frac{1}{2}$	8^{hd}	$7^{2\frac{1}{4}}$	Bejarano R	15.60
8Oct05 ^{7}OSA^{1}	Singletary	L	5	126	9	1	4^{hd}	$4\frac{1}{2}$	$3\frac{1}{2}$	6^{hd}	$8^{1\frac{1}{4}}$	Flores D R	8.70
8Oct05 ^{9}Kee^{6}	Ad Valorem	L	3	123	5	5	2^{hd}	$2\frac{1}{2}$	1^{hd}	3^{hd}	$9^{9\frac{1}{2}}$	Fallon K	37.25
4Sep05 LCH^{5}	Valixir-Ire		4	126	10	11	$9\frac{1}{2}$	$10^{2\frac{1}{2}}$	11	$10^{3\frac{1}{2}}$	$10\frac{3}{4}$	Soumillon C	10.40
1Oct05 ^{10}Bel^{4}	Sand Springs	L	5	123	4	4	$1\frac{1}{2}$	1^{hd}	9^{hd}	11	11	Bailey J D	18.80
2Oct05 ^{9}Bel^{1}	Funfair-GB	L	6	126	6	6	—	—	—	—	—	Prado E S	12.80

OFF AT 3:51 Start Good. Won driving. Course good.
TIME :23^{2}, :46^{3}, 1:11, 1:36 (:23.47, :46.68, 1:11.15, 1:36.10)

$2 Mutuel Prices:

2 – ARTIE SCHILLER	13.20	5.00	3.90
11 – LEROIDESANIMAUX-BRZ		3.80	3.00
8 – GORELLA-FR			6.00

$2 EXACTA 2–11 PAID $38.80 $2 TRIFECTA 2–11–8 PAID $504.00
$2 HEAD2HEAD 2VS.8VS.9WINNER2 PAID $3.70
$2 SUPERFECTA 2–11–8–3 PAID $7,021.00

B. c, (Apr), by El Prado–Ire – Hidden Light , by Majestic Light . Trainer Jerkens James A. Bred by Haras Du Mezeray SA (Ky).

Leroidesanimaux had run a brave and gritty race but clearly had been compromised by his foot problem, weakening late to lose to a horse he would have thrashed on his best day. You usually don't mind starting off a pick four with a $13.20 winner, but in this case I wondered whether Artie Schiller had been even that valuable. It was hard to believe that many pick-four players had singled Leroidesanimaux after the bar-shoe announcement, and Artie had been the second choice in the betting if not in my mind. Worse, since he had been only a B in my array, I had now lost all my C's the rest of the way.

With no B's in the Distaff, I had only my three A's—2-1 favorite Ashado, 9-2 co-second choice Happy Ticket, and 30-1 Pleasant Home. Ashado was a no-brainer—she was the defending Distaff winner, making her last start in a possible Hall of Fame career. Happy Ticket had run arguably as well as Ashado finishing second to her in the Beldame. I didn't really think Pleasant Home was as good as either of them, and she had started out as a C+ in my array, but the longer I had looked at her, the more the outside possibility of a victory at a huge price had convinced me to move her up to a B and eventually an A.

Making 1-2-3 "selections" for the Breeders' Cup races in *Daily Racing Form,* something I do only for the Triple Crown and Breeders' Cup, probably helped in this case. I never know what to do in a situation like this when the three horses I like are the two favorites and one interesting longshot: Put the two favorites on top because they're the likelier winners? Try to be a hero and put the longshot on top even though I think she has a lesser chance of victory than either of the favorites? I had compromised and put her in the middle, picking the race Ashado, Pleasant Home, Happy Ticket in print, so how could I make my published third choice an A and my published second choice only a B or a C? I'm glad that, unlike DRF's full-time handicappers, I don't have to wrestle with this issue more than four times a year.

With a few minutes to post for the Distaff, I realized I should probably bet the race separately instead of just rooting for my three A's, and this time I decided to dip a foot into all three intrarace pools to avoid a repeat of the unwise choice to play only superfectas in the Sprint. My problem was that I just didn't have any ideas beyond thinking that my three horses were the right ones and the rest of the race was a mess. Well, maybe I could get an Attila's Storm to run fourth this time, and I resorted to the coward's tool, the "all" button:

$20 exacta box 3,7,11	= $120
$20 exacta box 11/3,7	= $ 80
$2 trifecta part-wheel 3,7,11/3,7,11/all	= $132
$2 trifecta part-wheel 3,7,11/all/3,7,11	= $132
$1 super part-wheel 3,7,11/3,7,11/all/all	= $660
$1 super part-wheel 3,7,11/3,7,11/3,7,11/all	= $ 60
$1 super part-wheel 3,7,11/3,7,11/all/3,7,11	= $ 60

EIGHTH RACE
Belmont
OCTOBER 29, 2005

1⅛ MILES. (1.45^{2}) 22ND RUNNING OF THE EMIRATES AIRLINE BREEDERS' CUP DISTAFF. Grade I. Purse $2,000,000 FOR FILLIES AND MARES, THREE-YEAR-OLDS AND UPWARD. Northern Hemisphere three-year-olds, 120 lbs.; Older, 123 lbs.; Southern Hemisphere three-year-olds, 115 lbs.; Older, 123 lbs. $20,000 to pre-enter, $40,000 to enter, with guaranteed $2 million purse including nominator awards (plus Net Supplementary Fees, if any), of which 52% of all monies to the owner of the winner, 20% to second, 11% to third, 5.7% to fourth and 3% to fifth; plus stallion nominator awards of 2.6% of all monies to the winner, 1% to second and 0.55% to third and foal nominator awards of 2.6% of all monies to the winner, 1% to second and 0.55% to third. Closed with 14 pre-entries.

Value of Race: $1,834,000 Winner $1,040,000; second $400,000; third $220,000; fourth $114,000; fifth $60,000. Mutuel Pool $4,683,655.00 Exacta Pool $3,207,113.00 Trifecta Pool $2,778,062.00 Head2Head Pool $49,367.00 Superfecta Pool $941,048.00

Last Raced	Horse	M/Eqt.	A.	Wt	PP	St	¼	½	¾	Str	Fin	Jockey	Odds $1
9Oct05 ^{8}Kee^{2}	Pleasant Home	L	4	123	11	1	13	$12^{1\frac{1}{2}}$	11^{2}	1^{3}	$1^{9\frac{1}{4}}$	Velasquez C	30.75
1Oct05 ^{7}Bel^{3}	Society Selection	L	4	123	1	11	$10^{\frac{1}{2}}$	$9^{\frac{1}{2}}$	6^{hd}	$3^{1\frac{1}{2}}$	2^{nk}	Prado E S	11.80
1Oct05 ^{7}Bel^{1}	Ashado	L	4	123	3	7	6^{hd}	5^{hd}	$5^{\frac{1}{2}}$	$2^{\frac{1}{2}}$	$3^{2\frac{1}{4}}$	Velazquez J R	2.25
11Sep05 ^{9}Bel^{1}	Stellar Jayne	L b	4	123	2	8	2^{hd}	4^{hd}	2^{hd}	$5^{1\frac{1}{2}}$	$4^{2\frac{1}{4}}$	Dettori L	4.50
10Sep05 ^{7}Bel^{1}	In the Gold	L	3	120	10	13	11^{hd}	$11^{\frac{1}{2}}$	10^{hd}	6^{2}	5^{1}	Stevens G L	9.20
9Oct05 ^{8}Kee^{3}	Capeside Lady	L	4	123	13	2	1^{1}	$1^{\frac{1}{2}}$	$1^{1\frac{1}{2}}$	4^{2}	$6^{\frac{3}{4}}$	Decarlo C P	57.00
1Oct05 ^{9}Pha^{1}	Nothing But Fun	L f	3	120	4	12	12^{2}	$10^{2\frac{1}{2}}$	$8^{1\frac{1}{2}}$	$7^{2\frac{1}{2}}$	$7^{6\frac{1}{4}}$	Solis A	32.00
2Oct05 ^{7}OSA^{4}	Hollywood Story	L b	4	123	9	9	$7^{\frac{1}{2}}$	$7^{\frac{1}{2}}$	$12^{1\frac{1}{2}}$	10^{3}	$8^{3\frac{1}{4}}$	Valenzuela P A	30.25
1Oct05 ^{7}Bel^{4}	Sweet Symphony	L	3	120	12	10	9^{hd}	13	13	$9^{\frac{1}{2}}$	9^{4}	Bailey J D	7.70
2Oct05 ^{7}OSA^{3}	Island Fashion	L b	5	123	8	3	5^{1}	6^{hd}	$4^{\frac{1}{2}}$	$11^{2\frac{1}{2}}$	$10^{1\frac{1}{4}}$	Bejarano R	27.75
1Oct05 ^{7}Bel^{2}	Happy Ticket	L	4	123	7	5	$8^{1\frac{1}{2}}$	8^{1}	$3^{\frac{1}{2}}$	8^{1}	$11^{2\frac{1}{2}}$	Espinoza V	4.50
1Oct05 ^{9}Pha^{2}	Yolanda B. Too	L b	3	120	5	6	$3^{\frac{1}{2}}$	$2^{\frac{1}{2}}$	7^{hd}	12^{10}	$12^{24\frac{1}{4}}$	Coa E M	64.25
2Oct05 ^{7}OSA^{1}	Healthy Addiction	L b	4	123	6	4	4^{hd}	3^{1}	9^{hd}	13	13	Gomez G K	18.40

OFF AT 4:32 Start Good. Won driving. Track fast.

TIME :23^{1}, :46^{1}, 1:10^{3}, 1:35^{4}, 1:48^{1} (:23.33, :46.31, 1:10.74, 1:35.82, 1:48.34)

$2 Mutuel Prices:				
	11 – PLEASANT HOME	63.50	25.60	13.40
	1 – SOCIETY SELECTION		12.80	7.90
	3 – ASHADO			3.30

$2 EXACTA 11-1 PAID $692.00 $2 TRIFECTA 11-1-3 PAID $3,453.00
$2 HEAD2HEAD 6VS.12WINNER12 PAID $2.90
$2 SUPERFECTA 11-1-3-2 PAID $20,363.00

Dk. b or br. f, (May), by Seeking the Gold – Our Country Place , by Pleasant Colony . Trainer McGaughey III Claude R. Bred by Phipps Stable (Ky).

Pleasant Home was a glorious runaway winner, the race settled by the top of the stretch as she blasted away from the field. I didn't really get to appreciate the final yards of her historic triumph as I was watching the grueling duel for second place between Ashado and Society Selection. Had Ashado been able to gut it out, the $400,000 second-place prize would have narrowly made her the richest filly or mare in racing history. Closer to home, it would have given me a $40 exacta and a $1 superfecta. Alas, we both fell short by a neck, but Ashado won $220,000 for running third and at least I had $2 of the trifecta, my first cash of the day.

More important, a victory by an A at $63.50 had me in decent shape for what now had to be a good pick four. An A-A finish of Azamour or Bago with Saint Liam would give me a $5 pick four, while an A-B, B-A, or even B-B completion of the sequence would give me $1 of an undoubtedly healthy payoff.

With plenty of action and no strong opinions, I didn't need to bet on the Turf, and just rooted for Azamour and Bago for the possibility of a $5 pick four to Saint Liam. If they didn't get there, I still had Shirocco, Better Talk Now, Shakespeare, and Gun Salute to stay alive on the $1 tickets. . . .

NINTH RACE
Belmont
OCTOBER 29, 2005

1½ MILES. (Turf) (2.24^{1}) 22ND RUNNING OF THE JOHN DEERE BREEDERS' CUP TURF. Grade I. Purse $2,000,000 FOR THREE-YEAR-OLDS AND UPWARD. Northern Hemisphere Three-Year-Olds, 121 lbs.; Older, 126 lbs.; Southern Hemisphere Three-Year-Olds, 116 lbs.; Older, 125 lbs. All Fillies and Mares allowed 3 lbs. $20,000 to pre-enter, $40,000 to enter, with guaranteed $2million purse including nominator awards (plus Net Supplementary fees, if any), of which 52% of all monies to the owner of the winner, 20% to second, 11% to third, 5.7% to fourth and 3% to fifth; plus stallion nominator awards of 2.6% of all monies to thewinner, 1% to second and 0.55% to third and foal nominator awards of 2.6% of all monies to the winner, 1% to second and 0.55% to third. Closed with 15 pre-entries. Supplemental nominees: Shirocco (Ger) and Azamour (Ire).

Value of Race: $2,090,760 Winner $1,185,600; second $456,000; third $250,800; fourth $129,960; fifth $68,400. Mutuel Pool $5,411,517.00 Exacta Pool $3,286,824.00 Trifecta Pool $2,882,970.00 Head2Head Pool $44,307.00 Superfecta Pool $1,036,516.00

Last Raced	Horse	M/Eqt.	A.	Wt	PP	¼	½	1	1¼	Str	Fin	Jockey	Odds $1
2Oct05 LCH^{4}	Shirocco-Ger		4	126	2	2½	$2^{1\frac{1}{2}}$	2½	1½	1½	$1^{1\frac{3}{4}}$	Soumillon C	8.80
1Oct05 ^{8}Bel^{3}	Ace-Ire	L b	4	126	6	$9^{1\frac{1}{2}}$	8^{1}	4^{hd}	3½	$2^{1\frac{1}{2}}$	2^{nk}	Fallon K	16.40
10Sep05 Leo^{5}	Azamour-Ire	L	4	126	5	8^{hd}	11^{3}	8^{hd}	7½	$4^{2\frac{1}{2}}$	3¾	Kinane M J	3.65
2Oct05 LCH^{3}	Bago-FR		4	126	3	6½	5^{hd}	7^{hd}	6^{hd}	3^{2}	$4^{5\frac{3}{4}}$	Gillet T	4.50
1Oct05 ^{8}Bel^{2}	English Channel	L	3	121	10	4^{hd}	4^{1}	3^{1}	2½	5^{2}	5¾	Velazquez J R	11.40
24Sep05 ^{14}KD^{1}	Silverfoot	L	5	126	8	13	13	11½	8½	7^{2}	6^{1}	Bejarano R	31.00
10Sep05 ^{9}Bel^{1}	Better Talk Now	L bf	6	126	4	10½	9½	6½	5½	6^{1}	$7^{2\frac{1}{2}}$	Dominguez R A	8.70
15Oct05 ^{7}Haw^{1}	Gun Salute	L b	3	121	13	7½	7½	$10^{1\frac{1}{2}}$	9^{7}	8^{5}	8^{12}	Velasquez C	21.40
2Oct05 ^{8}OSA^{1}	Fourty Niners Son	L	4	126	9	$11^{2\frac{1}{2}}$	$10^{1\frac{1}{2}}$	9^{hd}	4^{hd}	9^{10}	$9^{11\frac{1}{4}}$	Nakatani C S	10.80
2Oct05 ^{8}OSA^{2}	Leprechaun Kid	L	6	126	12	5½	6½	13	$12^{2\frac{1}{2}}$	11^{3}	10¾	Gomez G K	39.75
2Oct05 ^{8}OSA^{3}	Laura's Lucky Boy	L	4	126	11	12^{2}	12½	12½	10½	10½	$11^{8\frac{3}{4}}$	Stevens G L	36.50
1Oct05 ^{8}Bel^{1}	Shakespeare	L	4	126	7	3^{hd}	3^{hd}	5^{hd}	11^{hd}	12^{7}	12^{8}	Bailey J D	3.90
10Sep05 ^{9}Bel^{11}	Shake the Bank	L b	5	126	1	13½	1^{7}	1^{2}	13	13	13	Turner T G	81.25

OFF AT 5:02 Start Good. Won driving. Course good.

TIME :23^{4}, :47^{4}, 1:13^{1}, 1:39^{2}, 2:05, 2:29^{1} (:23.95, :47.89, 1:13.20, 1:39.53, 2:05.05, 2:29.30)

$2 Mutuel Prices:				
	2 – SHIROCCO-GER	19.60	11.80	4.70
	6 – ACE-IRE		15.40	10.00
	5 – AZAMOUR-IRE			4.70

$2 EXACTA 2-6 PAID $296.50 $2 TRIFECTA 2-6-5 PAID $1,560.00
$2 HEAD2HEAD 3VS.4VS.7WINNER3 PAID $4.80
$2 SUPERFECTA 2-6-5-3 PAID $4,694.00

B. c, (Apr), by Monsun-Ger – So Sedulous , by The Minstrel . Trainer Fabre Andre. Bred by Baron Georg von Ullmann (Ger).

It only seemed to take forever to declare the race official and put up my pick-four probables:

3	Choctaw Nation	$71,498
11	Borrego	$22,375
13	Saint Liam	$17,303

With $1 tickets, I was looking at half those payoffs, or $8,651.50 with Saint Liam, $11,187.50 with Borrego, and $35,749 with Choctaw Nation, the horse I had moved into the B slot when Rock Hard Ten was scratched.

Now what? If Saint Liam or Borrego won, I would show a modest profit for the day after digging myself into a crater early on, and Choctaw Nation would be a score. If anyone else won, I would lose a little more than $5,000 for the afternoon, despite the $2 trifecta on the Distaff. Did it make sense to hedge? I couldn't bet all 10 of the ones I didn't have in the pick four, so I went the insanity-insurance route and just bet the three other horses I had considered elevating to B status in the late pick four instead of Choctaw Nation. So my final act of the day was to bet $300 to win on Flower Alley, Starcraft, and Oratorio, bringing my handle for the afternoon to a personal best of $9,818.

TENTH RACE
Belmont
OCTOBER 29, 2005

1¼ MILES. (1.58^{1}) 22ND RUNNING OF THE BREEDERS' CUP CLASSIC POWERED BY DODGE. Grade I. Purse $4,000,000 FOR THREE-YEAR-OLDS AND UPWARD. Northern Hemisphere Three-Year-Olds, 122 lbs.; Older, 126 lbs.; Southern Hemisphere Three-Year-Olds, 117 lbs.; Older, 126 lbs. All Fillies and Mares allowed 3 lbs. $40,000 to pre-enter, $80,000 to enter, with guaranteed $4million purse including nominator awards (plus Net Supplementary Fees, if any), of which 52% of all monies to the owner of the winner, 20% to second, 11% to third, 5.7% to fourth and 3% to fifth; plus stallion nominator awards of 2.6% of all monies to thewinner, 1% to second and 0.55% to third and foal nominator awards of 2.6% of all monies to the winner, 1% to second and 0.55% to third. Closed with 16 pre-entries. Supplemental nominee: Starcraft (NZ)

Value of Race: $4,291,560 Winner $2,433,600; second $936,000; third $514,800; fourth $266,760; fifth $140,400. Mutuel Pool $8,033,441.00 Exacta Pool $4,488,173.00 Trifecta Pool $4,222,093.00 Superfecta Pool $1,789,571.00

Last Raced	Horse	M/Eqt.	A.	Wt	PP	¼	½	¾	1	Str	Fin	Jockey	Odds $1
10Sep05 ^{10}Bel^{1}	Saint Liam	L b	5	126	12	4^{2}	4^{2}	5½	4½	1½	1^{1}	Bailey J D	2.40
1Oct05 ^{9}Bel^{4}	Flower Alley	L b	3	122	8	$3^{2\frac{1}{2}}$	3^{2}	4½	3½	2½	$2^{1\frac{1}{2}}$	Velazquez J R	10.00
24Sep05 ^{7}Haw^{4}	Perfect Drift	L	6	126	4	5^{1}	6½	6½	$6^{1\frac{1}{2}}$	5½	3^{nk}	Guidry M	14.50
24Sep05 ^{7}Haw^{1}	Super Frolic	L	5	126	6	10^{1}	7½	3^{hd}	5^{2}	4^{hd}	4^{nk}	Coa E M	69.25
1Oct05 ^{9}Bel^{2}	Suave	L b	4	126	7	$2^{1\frac{1}{2}}$	2^{2}	2^{1}	2½	$3^{1\frac{1}{2}}$	$5^{3\frac{1}{4}}$	Prado E S	16.40
1Oct05 ^{5}OSA^{3}	Choctaw Nation	L bf	5	126	2	13	12½	9^{hd}	8^{2}	8^{2}	$6^{1\frac{1}{4}}$	Espinoza V	13.00
24Sep05 ^{7}NEW^{1}	Starcraft-NZ	L f	5	126	13	$11^{1\frac{1}{2}}$	9½	8^{2}	7^{2}	7½	7½	Valenzuela P A	8.50
10Sep05 ^{10}Bel^{2}	Sir Shackleton	L	4	126	5	6½	10½	13	12½	11^{3}	8^{nk}	Castellano J J	36.50
1Oct05 ^{9}Bel^{3}	Sun King	L b	3	122	1	1^{hd}	1½	1½	1^{hd}	$6^{1\frac{1}{2}}$	9^{2}	Bejarano R	30.50
1Oct05 ^{9}Bel^{1}	Borrego	L	4	126	10	8^{hd}	11½	12½	10^{2}	10^{1}	$10^{1\frac{1}{2}}$	Gomez G K	2.60
15Oct05 NEW^{4}	Oratorio-Ire	L	3	122	3	7½	5½	7½	$9^{1\frac{1}{2}}$	$9^{1\frac{1}{2}}$	$11^{6\frac{1}{4}}$	Fallon K	9.40
8Sep05 DON^{8}	Jack Sullivan	L	4	126	9	12½	13	10½	13	12^{1}	12^{nk}	Dettori L	51.25
2Oct05 ^{8}WO^{1}	A Bit O'Gold	L	4	126	11	9½	8^{hd}	11^{2}	11½	13	13	Jones J	51.75

OFF AT 5:42 Start Good For All But SUPER FROLIC. Won driving. Track fast.

TIME :23^{4}, :47^{3}, 1:12^{1}, 1:36^{4}, 2:01^{2} (:23.98, :47.68, 1:12.23, 1:36.87, 2:01.49)

$2 Mutuel Prices:			
13 – SAINT LIAM	6.80	5.10	4.20
9 – FLOWER ALLEY		8.70	7.10
5 – PERFECT DRIFT			7.80

$2 EXACTA 13-9 PAID $62.00 $2 TRIFECTA 13-9-5 PAID $501.00
$2 SUPERFECTA 13-9-5-7 PAID $12,636.00

B. h, (Apr), by Saint Ballado – Quiet Dance, by Quiet American. Trainer Dutrow Richard E Jr. Bred by Edward P Evans (Ky).

The Breeders' Cup is one of the few remaining times when a multirace wager ends with the featured race of the day. In New York, the pick six initially ran from Races 3 through 8, and the last leg was often a stakes race. Now, even on Belmont or Travers Day, the pick four and pick six usually wrap up with a forgettable allowance race. (The change was made to push the start of the bet back by half an hour to attract more simulcast players from Western time zones.) So there was a nostalgic feeling watching Saint

Liam hold off Flower Alley by a length to win himself the Horse of the Year title and win me a dollar of the late pick four. Despite Saint Liam's victory, nobody picked six, and even the Players' Pool managed to come up with only four. The 38 combinations sold with five winners were worth $90,325 each.

Saint Liam had waged a gallant year-long campaign, facing top older horses from coast to coast, and his Classic victory and Horse of the Year title were a case of virtue rewarded. My eking out a profit for the day, however, was more a case of idiocy overcome. As I thought back over the afternoon's wagering, I almost lost count of the mistakes I had made: throwing out Intercontinental in the Filly and Mare Turf, betting the Sprint so poorly, making Artie Schiller a B instead of an A, neglecting to bet a nickel to win on Pleasant Home, and having the same $1 pick four to Saint Liam as I did to Borrego and Choctaw Nation. Still, there was more on the right than the left side of the ledger at day's end:

	LEDGER		
	10/29/05 – BELMONT PARK		
Race	**Bet Type**	**Bet**	**Return**
3rd	Pick Four	$ 1,320	$ 0
4th	Win	$ 200	$ 0
4th	Exacta	$ 146	$ 0
5th	Pick Six	$ 3,348	$ 0
6th	Win	$ 500	$ 0
6th	Superfecta	$ 1,080	$ 0
7th	Pick Four	$ 1,080	$ 8,651
8th	Exacta	$ 200	$ 0
8th	Trifecta	$ 264	$ 3,453
8th	Superfecta	$ 780	$ 0
10th	Win (savers)	$ 900	$ 0
TOTAL		$ 9,818	$12,104

I checked my account balance on the way out of the track to confirm that my math was correct and that I had indeed made a $2,286 profit on the afternoon. I then had a panicky moment when my balance was only $124 higher than it had been at the start of the day. What had happened to the other $2,162? Had I only had the tri in the Distaff for $1? Had I accidentally bet $1,000 instead of $300 to win on those three savers in the Classic? Had the Saint Liam pick four paid $2,162 less than I thought it had?

And then I remembered my partner. Good old Uncle Sam had taken exactly $2,162 out of the $8,652 pick-four return, a "25 percent" withholding that actually amounted to 94.5 percent of my $2,286 profit for the afternoon.

Still, how unhappy could I be? Breeders' Cup Day had been my 49th birthday, and I had spent it at Belmont Park, enjoying both spectacular horse racing and parimutuel thrills and chills on an epic scale. It had all been pretty exotic.